GW01607466

THE UNFINISHED STORY

H. R. PLASTOW

A VERY PRACTICAL APPROACH TO **THE SPIRIT WORLD, HEALING, HAUNTINGS AND E.S.P.** BEING AN ACCOUNT OF EXPERIENCES OF THE AUTHOR AND HIS FAMILY, THROUGHOUT THEIR LIVES.

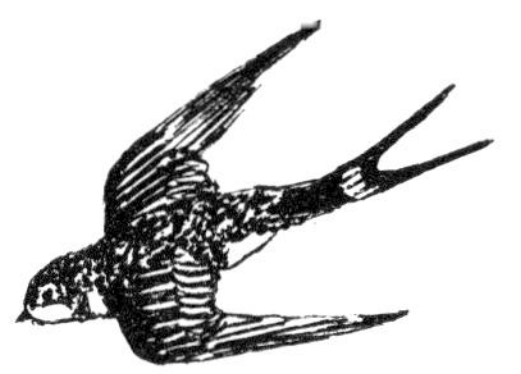

'Publications – H. R. Plastow.'

First published in 1985

ISBN 0 9501908 4 5

Published by
'Publications – H. R. Plastow.'

Typeset by Waveney Typesetters, Norwich, Norfolk
Printed and Bound in Great Britain
by Anchor Brendon Ltd., of Tiptree, Essex.

AN AWARENESS

A young lad first experiences 'The Unusual' when ten years old; again while growing up in war time, and then periodically throughout life. Somewhere along the way this lad (the author), realises that these experiences should be recorded for others to appreciate, and even benefit by.

An injury results in a meeting with a healer, and a 'Humorous Spirit'. The tragic death of a brother is followed by direct voice contact (from him) on two occasions. Healing takes care of people, and a badly injured horse. Apparitions are witnessed by up to four people together, and separately; and the members of the family are also involved.

This account is quite unique, and contrary to popular belief, almost all of the happenings have caused no alarm, and have often been helpful.

The manner of some of the manifestations makes them so obvious, and their variety is so astounding, that one might seriously wonder if the whole sequence was planned by a higher intelligence? You must form your own conclusions.

'The Unfinished Story' is so called, because the incidents continue, and probably will while the author is alive. The account also describes some 'Ordinary' events in the lives of the author, and his family, to give background and humour to the experiences.

From childhood we were taught that there is a life after death. The experiences (described in this book) have convinced the author beyond reasonable doubt that these teachings are true, although we cannot fully understand what form this life takes.

My sincere thanks to the family, and all good friends who have inevitably become involved with the paranormal, in the experiences described in this book, and for their more material help in bringing it into being. Also to Alethea for her interest and encouragement.

H.R.P.

AUTHOR'S NOTE

I believe that most things in life have a purpose, although we may not always appreciate this.

It is my wish throughout the pages of this book to encourage a more ordinary, and less apprehensive view of the spirit world. From Chapter 3 onwards, the 'Supernatural' occurrences become a part of everyday life, and one does not feel any fear in their manifestation. However, quite the reverse was experienced in the incident concerning 'The Monk', Chapter 2, and to a lesser degree in the happenings described in Chapter 1. These two early contacts with the 'Supernatural' (being beyond known physical laws), no doubt served in a positive way to make me more aware of 'The World of Spirit', in the years that followed.

The occurrences described here span about fifty years of my life, and are faithfully recorded. The variety of manifestations is very surprising, and collectively they disprove just about every theory, that there is no connection between the supernatural, and life after death.

It has been suggested that apparitions – ghosts, are a mirror of the mind, and that they are **not seen by more than one person**; thus the apparition is explained as being of **the beholder's own making**. In this record of events these explanations are disproved **not once**, but **several times**, and in a most positive manner – Chapter 15 – 'The Little Old Lady', is witnessed by two persons, separately; and two people travelling together, but in different years; and all describing the same old lady with the same stance, and in the same location along the road. These sightings perhaps more than any, completely preclude the possibility of **mirror of the mind**. 'The Twice Vanishing Impala' (an apparition), is witnessed by three men, at the same time, and again is very informative.

In Chapter 6 one reads of direct voice contact from my brother, who was killed; and this was heard by three people together. In Chapter 8, I claim there is proof of life after death, or the nearest thing to it that we are likely to obtain in this life. With the wildest stretch of imagination, there would appear to be no other explanation.

'The Unfinished Story' is a record to date (1985), of a lifetime's fascinating experiences. They will occur anywhere, and be completely unexpected, and have no association with politics, colour or creed.

Perhaps, in a simple way, and with no particular religious beliefs, or preconceived ideas; we have been privileged to be involved in events which bring us nearer to an understanding of the truth.

H.R.P.

CONTENTS

ILLUSTRATIONS

FOREWORD

Henry Plastow is an engineer and designer who has specialised in machine tools, and then concentrated on Steam Models. His designs together with castings for the construction of large scale Steam Traction Models have been sold world wide, and his book on the building and running of such models, is a definitive work.

The paranormal is a subject that seems to be of interest to all thinking people. All those with an enquiring turn of mind must find themselves puzzled by events that do not lend themselves to a logical explanation. **This book** has been written because a skilled engineer, keeping an open mind has set down the details of various happenings, in his personal experience; and where I have been concerned, I can vouch for the accuracy of his writing.

Henry is now in middle age, as I am myself, and we come on to common ground in believing that some things seem to be preordained and not entirely within our own control. He has packed a good many different experiences into his working life, and an unusual chain of events took him, and family, from a house in Enfield when I first got to know him, to a substantial and very handsome old rectory, standing in its own grounds in Suffolk. It almost goes without saying that the rectory was haunted, although the manifestations seem to have more or less ceased now. (See Conclusion.) This old house has always seemed to have an atmosphere of peace and tranquility.

It was motoring to the rectory a few years ago that I saw the ghost of an old lady which is described in this book. I was quite unaware at that time, that what I saw was a ghost. I just saw an old lady who seemed not to move from her bent position, when I passed her. I was somewhat concerned for her safety as the road is quite narrow at this point and there seemed no obvious place where she could have come from, or gone to. By the time I had turned this over in my mind I was past her, but the impression was vivid and I was unable to dismiss this. You may imagine my astonishment when later that evening, Henry started to describe the event exactly as I had seen it.

The occurrence related in Chapter 28 regarding the Impala is accurately recorded. Henry, myself and Jaap Seegers (a man of great experience to whom the various antelope were immediately identifiable), were watching when the Impala disappeared.

The knowledge of our own universe gradually increases, and some understanding of its size and age is comprehended. The time and space we live in started many millions of years ago at the beginning of creation, and perhaps will continue for all time.

The immensity and age of our universe is difficult for the human mind to grasp, and to consider that there might be another existence besides our own must be even harder to accept. Our minds cope with our own dimension and time, and only with difficulty perceive any other intelligence around us.

In the fullness of time I expect everything will be explained. In the meantime we must accept that the Universe is a very strange place.

R. W. May, A.M.I.E.

Chapter 1

AN INTRODUCTION TO THE MYSTERIOUS

A basis for progress, understanding, and research of 'Spiritual' matters.

Several times over the years I have been tempted to record those of my experiences, which cannot be explained in the usual manner.

I have come to believe that there is unquestionably, life after death, and I am convinced that there is a wealth of help and guidance available to us from persons in which I choose to call 'Class A'.

There have been many descriptions of hauntings, and spiritual matters, over the years, most of which conjure up fear of the unknown, doubt, and often ridicule of those persons who by their very nature may be able to perceive, or experience more than others. I have often been frustrated by the conceit of some of the general public, who are so emphatic in their conviction that ghosts, or apparitions, are only a myth.

At this present time, there is becoming an awareness of such matters, and one sometimes hears an admission that – yes there may be 'Something'. Unfortunately, the majority of investigations and research are carried out in a most unsuitable way – the scientific approach. Anyone who has had any spiritual experiences and begins to have some small understanding of them, will probably agree that a technical approach is just not going to produce any results at all. I have observed that spiritually developed people are often the most simple, unassuming persons, and I believe it is only because they have humble minds, not filled with any preconceived notions, that they are therefore receptive. Recently I listened to an interview, in which a man of science – a psychologist expressed the view that modern man had lost his psychic ability. It was stated that Neanderthaloid man had a high degree of psychic development, because he trusted first and sought proof afterwards.

My family and I have never actively sought any association with any religious or spiritual groups, and therefore the experiences that we have undergone have generally come to us unsought. Having said this, I have read a certain amount regarding such matters and recall various attempts to explain spiritual happenings, and from these, certain ideas have been expressed in print, several times. A common belief is that it is possible during sleep for the spiritual body of a living creature to depart from its physical body and travel, often appearing in an entirely different place. Indeed, there are many dreams that will convince one of the possibility of this. Many people have had the experience of having been to a place before, and this is a possible explanation, but nothing more. One reads various theories, and if we accept life after death, it is unlikely that we shall know the whole truth of the matter until our lives on this earth are ended. This thought may provoke a certain amount of unease; however, I have felt for some time that there is far too much mystery and apprehension associated with spiritual matters, and it seems to me that this should not be so. After all, there is usually a logical explanation for most things, and recently I have come to believe that I may have at least, a very feasible answer, and in fact illustrated by our cat. This described later.

I think it is only with trust, and the near complete removal of disbelief that it is possible for spirit persons to communicate, and only in this way is it possible to receive help, or to learn. (Refer to the consultation before buying The Old Rectory.) If we accept or even think it possible that there is life after death, then it would seem likely that there is a higher form of intelligence in this uplifted form of life than that which we experience here. Let us now consider this intelligence as being akin to that of a professor or an instructor, knowing infinitely more than his pupils, otherwise why would he be teaching? Can we imagine the present attitude to spirit life, applied to this particular instance. Firstly, the pupils would be in utter disbelief that the teacher existed; secondly, they would attempt to discredit or ridicule everything that the teacher told them, or were shown. You might well say – what a ridiculous situation. Why then should it be any different when we are privileged to be shown sights, sounds and the working of senses, which may be beyond our normal comprehension, and yet may well be a means of leading us to a knowledge of higher things.

In the chapters that follow, there will be various accounts of happenings, one which must come close to proof of life after death, because it concerns four living people, and in different places, and my own brother who had recently been killed. There will be other examples in which I and my wife have sought guidance, and where help was very definitely given; much in the manner that Kings, in olden times are reputed to have consulted the astrologers.

It is my intention to relate accurately, all of the occurrences, and illustrate the various points which I have made. Certainly, it will be very easy to show how one may obtain help from those of the spirit. In relating to you the experiences of our ordinary family, it is my hope that the reader may take a more ordinary view of what has been for centuries a most extraordinary subject.

As I pass through the years, I shall mention various places and people by their exact names, some with whom I have completely lost touch. However, I am quite sure that none will object to being mentioned in this book as they will know if they read it, that I am relating the exact truth.

Bearing in mind my belief that spiritual progress and understanding can only be brought about by a mind completely without preconceived ideas, or nearly so, I ask the reader to accept what is recounted as fact, and not waste time in trying to find inadequate explanations. To take these occurrences at their face value, to accept what is fact as such, and to question as we do, in the chapter, the validity of occurrences which could have another explanation, i.e. The Glass of Port which Moved. In this frame of mind, it is possible then, to learn. No one is suggesting that the reader develops unlikely beliefs, or attempts to give the spirit world more credulity than is actually indicated.

At the risk of being thought to be presumptuous, I am going to express my theories as to the explanation of hauntings, and supernatural matters, which defy any normal understanding. Let us consider that the mind is the key to the whole matter. Indeed, is this not the substance of the soul, which lives on after death, and is the all important factor which determines what sort of people we are.

Most of us have seen, read about, or experienced some form of E.S.P., and it is unlikely that anyone would question that these extra-sensory powers emanate from anywhere other than the mind. The number of known forms of E.S.P. may be considerable. I can remember my old maths master, Mr. Tate telling us that there was considerable evidence that the ancient Egyptians could project thought messages over great distances. I must confess that I never questioned this statement, and expect that this was indicated by the paintings, or writings in the tombs. Certainly, I am in no doubt now, that this is not an uncommon occurrence.

From observation, it would seem that what I call mental projection is triggered off in a manner, which we do not understand. However, I find that the forces from the mind seem to be projected when the normal pattern of things is interrupted. One thinks of a tune, and a friend starts to whistle it – a very common happening, with basic similarities to others that I will relate. I believe that because the mental process of formulating a tune was carried out, but not completed by actually projecting it as sound, that the force went in another direction, and was projected mentally, for someone to receive. An example of which I have recently become aware, strengthens this belief. I often formulate what I am going to say to my wife, and yet not having spoken, and she will often say "Pardon", or "Did you say something?". Again the force not being used in its normal direction, and being projected in another. The same thing occurs in my case, in the limited amount of spiritual healing that I have attempted. I 'WILL' my hands to lift, without allowing them to do so, and some type of force is created, which is beyond normal explanation. This described in the text.

After I married, it became an extremely common occurrence when visiting my mother, for her to say that she had got the kettle on as she was expecting us. Not a case of making a pot of tea, and keeping it hot, but knowing almost exactly when we would arrive.

There are many forms of E.S.P., – one is entering a room, and immediately is aware that it is empty, or conversely that there is someone in it. This is a common enough event. I recall seeing a programme, on which a blind person was able to tell colour when touching an object. Some years ago, I experimented with two of my daughters when they were young, and found that it was possible with my eyes shut, to tell which one of them had come up to me. I would not care to try and explain this, other than perhaps that they may have their own distinctive aura (like a magnetic field), and somehow one can sense it. Obviously enough, these powers whatever they be, come from the mind. The mind must be perhaps the most brilliant force ever created. Certainly, we are not even at the beginning of learning of all its potential. It is a fact that many of modern man's creations, however clever they may appear, are often attempts to achieve some of the functions of the human mind.

Most of us have had that enlightening experience associated with the memory bank of the mind, of suddenly being transported back through the years, to an incident such as one I recall, of fishing for Perch along the banks of a canal at Ponders End (as a boy), and this brought about by the sound of the wind in the grasses on a summer's day, or perhaps the hum of the insects, acting as the key to the memory of the mind. To be taken back to a first romance in a similar manner, merely because of a particular sound, sight or smell can be equally surprising and pleasing. It seems that regardless of whether we have a good memory or not in the normal sense, that the store of memories, indeed the record of one's life is there, in its entirety, and it is only one's ability to tap this source which decides whether we have a good or a bad memory.

Returning to man's latest creations, one will realise that many are designed to carry out some of the functions of the human mind, and its senses. This is true enough of computers, which are intended to be a super-mind, although of course need programming. Video machines, televisions, projectors of sound and vision, all carry out functions of the mind. The point I am making, is that many modern pieces of equipment are based on extensions or activities of the mind, and I put it to you, that the key to the whole matter of life on this earth and in the life beyond, is indeed the mind, and that all matters of E.S.P. and supernatural occurrences may well be attributable to this. The mind is the key.

I have long held the (not uncommon) belief that many hauntings are associated with live people, and creatures, rather than the so called dead ones. I was privileged to have this belief confirmed for me, very conveniently, just as I was about to commence writing this book. We have a small cat of twelve years, and this is an affectionate animal, but of a rather nervous disposition. My daughter Julie was sitting down attending to paperwork, when she saw that the cat had come alongside her, stood up on its hind legs and reached up to touch her, to be stroked, as it commonly does. Nothing unusual about this, other than the fact that the cat was sound asleep in a cardboard box a couple of yards from her. See photograph. She mentioned this to my wife and myself, then two days later, I happened to open the kitchen door; this leads through a passage to a door to the backyard. Immediately, I saw our cat run through from the back door, hesitate in its nervous manner, look back quickly over its shoulder as if to change its mind, and then run onwards into the same room, where it normally sleeps in its cardboard box. Again nothing very strange about this perhaps, other than the fact that I knew for certain that I had let the cat out into the yard only a few minutes previously. Also, it had run through the back door, **which was closed**. On checking, I confirmed that the cat was very definitely not inside the house – at least, not in its physical form. I can assure the reader that the detail of the cat and its mannerisms were such that unless I had been aware that she was not inside the house, I would not have given it a second thought. Perhaps the reader will humour my belief that a message was being passed on to me at an opportune moment, and which in fact has confirmed my theories, which are expressed in this book. See photograph 2. We know it is fact that my daughter and I, saw the cat, and also that it was carrying out exactly the same activities that it normally does; but what we cannot know is whether we received a visual, or a mental picture.

For those who have not witnessed any form of manifestation, the projections of the cat's image may be somewhat difficult to accept. Please refer to the last paragraph in the addendum to Chapter 26, and to the chapter – 'India – Land of Mystery'; where a more advanced

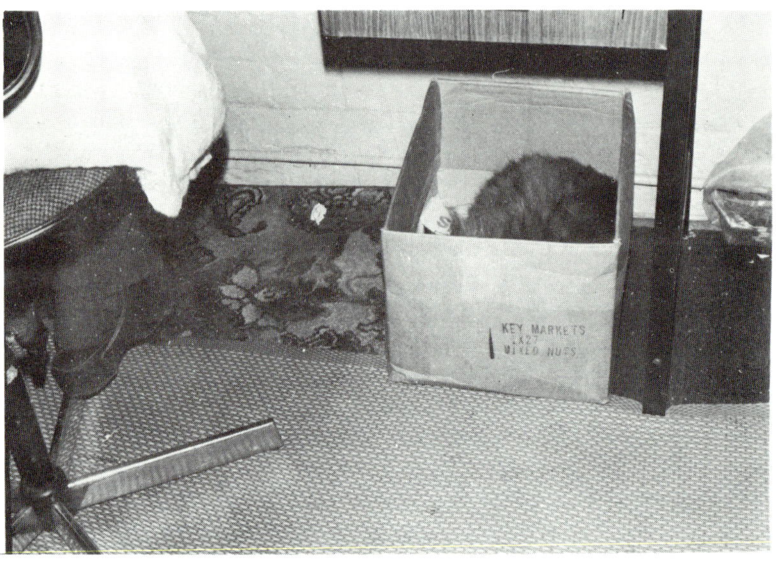

Cat 'Tibby' asleep in cardboard box.

Cat by Aga cooker.

form of 'Projection' – 'Aware Projection', is almost certainly described.

So many experiences are explained away by coincidence, or 'Just one of those things'. When I consider what a remarkable coincidence it is that I have thought about writing this book, on two previous occasions, and indeed made notes; yet on the first occasion that I seriously decide to write, that first a theory comes to me, to explain various happenings, and then within a few days, mental projection is illustrated to my daughter; and then, within a couple of days is corroborated for myself. Reasonably, one must assume that it would take a rare stretch of coincidence for mental projection to be illustrated to us, at the right time, and being the first time in my 57 years, and in such an obvious manner.

One learns, or should do, after a number of experiences, that those in a superior existence are trying to help, and we must throw aside the veil of distrust, and conceit, and benefit from their efforts.

A basis then for research and understanding of spiritual matters, must be the ability to accept life after death – to accept that there are spiritual visitations and happenings, although we cannot understand them, and then to go forward with a receptive, and trusting mind, when proofs may well be available. Undoubtedly it will be difficult for those of a scientific mind to discount their knowledge, but remember, the knowledge of the scientist concerns only this present life, and the laws of physics which apply to it.

BLESSED ARE THE MEEK, FOR THEY SHALL INHERIT THE EARTH.

Chapter 2

A FIRST EXPERIENCE AND THE WAR

I think my upbringing was relatively strict, although in the years before the Second World War there was much more general respect throughout the community; respect for the church, one's parents, one's employer, and certainly for one's appearance. Perhaps the fact that I had to go to church three times on most Sundays, may have turned me away from a conventional form of Christianity. Gradually, I formed my own beliefs and views, modelled from life and experience, rather than from those based on traditional ideas.

* * *

At the time of my first unexplainable occurrence, I was about ten years old and living in a house in Carpenter Gardens, Winchmore Hill – this would probably have been 1937. In the usual way, with children in those days, I went to bed at about half past eight. It was still full light, being summer time. My bedroom was the smaller one to the right of the landing, at the top of the stairs. The curtains were drawn, although there was still a fair amount of light inside the room. I must have been in bed for a quarter of an hour or so, and was still awake, when I both heard and sensed someone, or something coming quietly up the stairs. I felt sure this could not be my parents, whose heavier footfalls I would have recognised. As the quiet footsteps reached the top of the landing, and came towards my room, there were two distinct knocks on my bedroom door. Although quite terrified, I called out "Come in"; what else could I have done? Now, this particular door had a peculiarity, in that one could turn the handle, but the door would not open unless the handle was lifted at the same time. I believe it must have been fortunate for me that my unknown visitor was not aware of this peculiarity, as immediately after my call of "Come in", I heard the door handle turn and the door rattle a few times as an attempt was made to open it. Someone braver than myself at that moment, might have opened the door, but I felt safer where I was, and after a long time, sleep must have overtaken me. In the morning I asked if any of the family had come upstairs shortly after I had gone to bed, and they said very definitely that they had not.

My brother Stan (a regular in the R.A.F.), often spent part of his leaves taking me fishing, until in the early part of the war, he was drafted to India. I can still remember the fascinating lake where he and his friend Ray Peck would catch quite sizeable Carp, and I would try to follow their example. I saw the same lake some fifteen years ago; it was then completely surrounded by houses, and I understand that at that time, there were complaints about the mosquitoes coming off the water. I can well remember the attraction of this place, no-one seemed to own it, and to get to it after a long bike ride, we went across several fields, crossed over various ditches and eventually came to the lake, often shrouded in the mists of early morning as we started to fish. There were a couple of small islands, quite a large mass of bullrushes, and reeds all around the fringes, which no doubt contributed to the not too pleasant odour which we associated with Boxes Lake.

Once we had reached the water, there was only one small cottage in sight in the far distance. In the years we went there, I cannot recall ever seeing a soul after we had left the road. How would one find such a place today unspoiled, unknown to all but a few, and full of fine Carp waiting to be caught?

As boys we did quite a bit of fishing. I remember on one occasion catching a very heavy fish, with no fight in it at all. In fact it was a hundred foot rope that had fallen into the River Lea, from a passing barge.

* * *

I joined the cubs, and then the scouts, becoming involved in the usual things, camping and scout shows (see photograph), until the war curtailed our activities.

During the blitz, some of us scouts helped by carrying out fire watching duty, there being a fair amount of incendiary, and high explosive bombs dropped at that time. Three fire-watchers were on duty together, and often including Father Mathews, our Vicar of Holy Trinity Church, Winchmore Hill. He was a good man, always ready to help, always cheerful, and would often play the vestry piano to entertain us if we were not on duty for the first part of the night,

The author (second from left), as a cub, takes part in the Scout Show. Circa 1936.

and sometimes finishing with a favourite, Handel's 'Largo' before we got down to sleep.

The early years of one's life often model what is to follow, and war time is not the best environment to grow up in. Our immediate area received a very fair quota of Hitler's offerings, although fortunately some quite remarkably, landing in the best possible location – the aerial mine falling in the Stationer's Playing Field, harming no-one. The one thousand pound high explosive bomb landing in the Winchmore Hill School playing field at the bottom of the road, making a hole big enough to take two trolley buses, but no-one being killed. These were near miracles, which left lots of blast damage, but no heartache.

Several friends and I became adept at replacing doors, and sealing windows, becoming good friends of the council workmen, who just could not keep up with the repeated repairs. Often complete door pillars were split from top to bottom, or blasted out entirely, making repairs somewhat awkward and lengthy.

One important and 'Urgent' job I remember doing for one family was to repair their toilet seat, which had been blasted into several pieces. These happenings for a period, became commonplace and no doubt we became hardened to the effects of war, being young, and perhaps not worrying too much as long as the bombs did not come too close.

We experienced the Doodle Bugs, and after a while did not worry as long as the engine stopped fairly close overhead, when the flying bomb would glide away from us. However, there was one alarming exception to this when one passed overhead, continued some distance, and then curved round to fly back towards us. Fortunately for us, but not for others, it fell before it reached our immediate area.

It is possible to get used to most things, and also to tire of sleeping in an Anderson air raid shelter, and so like many, we returned to sleeping in the house and 'Chancing it'.

As technology progressed, the Doodle Bugs were replaced by rockets – one of these unfortunately, making a direct hit on our road during one night, also blowing up the gas main. I awoke to find the complete ceiling had come down, and to be choked with the dust of ages that fell with it. Going to a back window, I looked out to see houses flattened and some on fire, and could hear someone continually calling – "Help, help". We were lucky to escape unhurt, the roof, doors and windows were off but this was nothing compared to the considerable death and injury that occurred to our friends and neighbours, just a few doors down the road. Perhaps for a while, us youngsters became older than our years.

I remember that on coming downstairs, in darkness, immediately after the explosions; that the door to the living room puzzled me considerably. I was able to put my hands through the top half of the door, as it appeared to be open, but something was stopping my legs. It is strange what an explosion will do, sometimes blasting one object to pieces, whilst another right alongside, remains unharmed. In the case of the door, it had been blown off its hinges, turned on its side and replaced across the doorway.

Pages of my mother's recipe book littered ours, and the adjacent gardens. This was a fawn coloured exercise book which had contained her secrets for wine making, at which she was an expert. Left on the living room table, the blast had reduced it to individual pages and scattered them far and wide. It had been a common sight to see an enamel bath, full of wine in the making, and with yeast spread on toast floating on the top, in the old-fashioned way. We had no time for picking up recipe pages then, and the rain soon finished off the destruction that the blast had started, as the ink ran making the pages unreadable.

One vivid memory concerns a 'Red Worm'. The emergency services and those that manned them, were quite wonderful. We had no water or gas for several days and so, almost immediately, there were vehicles on the scene and hot drinks and sandwiches were being dispensed to all, quite free. Tea was much appreciated, in unusual quantities, after experiencing the choking dust that is present when ceilings are blasted down.

Soon the Winchmore Hill School was being used as an emergency dining hall. Services were obviously stretched to the limit of supplies, and labour, although one might never have realised this but for one live red worm which wriggled out of the lettuce of my salad; I remember pushing it aside and finished the meal with hardly a thought. I could not do that now.

What wonderfully spontaneous help we experienced in those days, there even being mobile showers for us to clean up after trying to get our homes into some sort of useable order.

* * *

Another vivid memory:– The council workmen, and other services could not keep up with the repairs, and so within a few days we were given an enormous tarpaulin sheet to cover the roof, and keep out the rain. My school friends were soon on the scene to get this into place. (My father had died in 1941.) One of the lads – Allen Tyrrel, always one to see the funny side of any situation, and a good climber; was near the rooftop pulling up the tarpaulin, when he chanced to look down and saw my sister in the bath. Of course all the upper ceilings had gone completely; his view was unrestricted, and he erupted into laughter, making a ribald comment. I remember being unable to see the funny side of the situation, at the time, making some unpleasant remark. However, one must never lose a sense of humour.

One may wonder what part these events play in a book concerning E.S.P. and the supernatural. Firstly, I am trying to show that a background such as this is hardly likely to produce a soft, imaginative outlook on life, to strengthen the validity of our experiences, and secondly, and all important, to emphasise the horrors of war, brought about by man's lust for power, and gain, and that there is a lesson to be learned in trying to prevent it happening in the future. Fourteen people being killed, and a number badly injured, on that fateful night seemed lesson indeed.

H. Copnall

'The Monk'.

Chapter 3

A SECOND EXPERIENCE 'THE MONK'

Like many other lads, I helped the family economy by doing a paper round. At the particular time I am describing, I had been delivering papers in the Winchmore Hill area for some long while. In fact, I did this throughout most of the war. My morning round started from the newsagents at the top of Station Road, Winchmore Hill, and I would deliver papers right the way through Broad Walk and various turnings off it. Then I would take a turning to the left, before I reached The Bourne, and put papers through the doors as I made my way homewards.

On the morning I am recalling, I delivered papers to some of the big houses as I entered Broad Walk, I turned right into one of the smaller roads, and then cut through to a road running down to Grovelands Park. As I pulled into the curb facing down towards the park, I swung my leg over the bike and turned up the hill to deliver a paper. My bike was slightly past the gateway of the house to which I was delivering; I turned at an angle to walk back to the gate; just to the left of this I saw something which scared me more than anything else throughout the rest of my life. Even at the height of the blitz in the war, I can never remember experiencing such fear as I did then. It is said that one's hair stands on end, but because of the balaclava helmet which I usually wore, this would have been impossible. However, I have never experienced since, such an intense tingling at the roots of my hair.

What I saw was without any doubt, an apparition; it was a very tall monk or man of the church – tall and very heavily built and who towered above me to an alarming degree. The cassock and hood, and facial details were amply plain enough to leave no doubt as to what one was looking at. As I stood rooted to the spot, this apparition moved towards me, without the slightest sound, at which I was so terrified that I turned, threw my leg over the bike and pedalled away furiously without delivering the paper. I might add here that I never again delivered papers in the same order, and always arranged that I reached this spot in full light from then on.

Now, I can hear the 'Doubting Thomases' trying to explain this matter away. Of course, those persons who are used to being about before light on cold, damp winter mornings may well think they have all the materials necessary to offer a full explanation. There were plenty of trees and shrubs in the area, which dripped eerily and incessantly on this bitterly cold winter's morning, before it was fully light. I was not very old, and so, the doubters might have imagined me to be in a permanent state of fear whilst carrying out my morning round. However, I think I was no different to other young lads, in that I did not get numb with cold morning after morning, for any pleasure it gave; I wanted to get my round finished as quickly as possible and did not give my mind to dreaming. I can remember being so thoroughly impressed and scared by it all that I described the whole incident to an oldish lady who I often met on the round, who also delivered papers; I believe she came from a newsagents called Tidy's which was located alongside the Green at the end of Broad Walk.

To the doubters, I would say that one experience such as this will convince them beyond any doubt that there is something – although maybe nothing further than this.

Recalling my theories that all spiritual visitations may well be brought about by the projection of the mind, whether it be from persons or creatures, either living or (what we term) dead. I will refer to the incident when I myself saw our cat run through the door, hesitate and then carry on – although at the time it was outside in the grounds. Also, to the cat standing up on its hind legs and patting my daughter, as it often does, and yet at this time it was sound asleep in its box. The reader will note that in both cases, this mental projection (which I feel it is), takes exactly the same path or reproduces the same actions as it has commonly done. Now, let us come back to the monk or man of the church. My eyes were drawn to the face and general upper part of the body. Being close to the apparition; unless I had purposely looked down, which I did not; I would have been unaware of the details from say, ankle level down to the ground. What overawed me was the enormous height of this being, probably eight feet and big built too. Now, this height may be relatively easy to understand. Apparitions mostly seem to be recorded to take exactly the same path or carry out the same actions as they have previously done, and do nothing more. For example, I have rarely heard of anyone meeting an apparition and having a discussion with it, although it is not uncommon for a discussion to be carried out with a person in spirit, through a medium.*

The house to which I was delivering, was on the side of a hill, and in fact the road slopes steeply down to Grovelands Park, the road being a cul-de-sac. Therefore, it is extremely likely that the ground at the point of the visitation was once a great deal higher, and was only levelled when the present road was being made, and the houses were being built. If therefore, I had been braver and had cared to linger, it is likely that I would have seen that there was a gap between the reverend gentleman and the ground. I firmly believe that what I saw was the mental projection of a person in spirit retracing his steps over a path he had used many times in the past. I say in spirit because of his attire, and the fact that it is unlikely that a living person would project this type of image. I am quite sure that when this apparition moved towards me, after being stationary, that it was not with any conscious intention of frightening me, it was merely retracing steps carried out probably many times before.

I feel that many apparitions can be explained in this way, although there are other types for which I will attempt to give an explanation in another chapter. One often hears a theory put forward that these apparitions are trapped on the atmosphere or the surroundings, in some manner which no one can explain. I personally consider that this explanation is most unlikely to be correct. Perhaps it might be possible for some force to retain a fixed image, much as a magnet will hold iron filings in a particular pattern when the magnetic force is applied; but, how it would be possible for detailed, and moving objects to re-appear by being trapped on the atmosphere (a variable entity), is something I am not able to accept.

Grovelands Park is fairly extensive, and even today is a well wooded area. It seems quite possible that in years gone by a monastery or a church might have stood close by. Certainly, monks, like paper boys, did not enjoy long lie-ins on cold winter mornings. They would have been about their chores at the same early hours.

Apparitions always seem to appear at the same time of the day, season and year, and could well be projected from the memory bank (of living or spirit person or creature), rather than by any conscious effort to arrange these regular appearances.

I described my paper round experience to a school friend – Willie Neech, because of his interest in such things. He was keen to investigate the matter, but no doubt I had seen enough. I did not get involved, and from that day to this, I have never sought such experiences; those that I, and my family have been privileged to witness, simply happening.

*The following experience was described to me by an ex Metropolitan policeman, stationed in the Tottenham area a good number of years ago. It was common enough for the police to see, and pass the time of day with the nuns from a local convent. On this particular evening, a constable (of 7 or 8 years' service) was starting his beat, and had just left the station, when a nun appeared alongside him, turned to look towards him, and carried on walking beside him until about a hundred and fifty yards from the station, she turned and walked through the wall. This experience left such a profound impression on the constable that he did his best not to walk past this spot again. After this incident, enquiries were made and it was discovered that in years gone by, there had been a gateway at the point where the apparition had passed through the wall.

Although, in this instance I am not allowed to disclose the name of any person involved, this occurrence is well worth mentioning because it is another good example of an apparition (projection) travelling on the same path, and carrying out the same actions that **its source** had carried out many times before. In many such incidents, the apparition appears exactly as a normal person, and would cause no comment or apprehension, until the unusual ability to walk through the wall (in this instance), was demonstrated. Bearing this in mind, it is likely that **many** people have seen apparitions and been completely unaware of it.

Chapter 4

GOOD YEARS: DANCES, ARMY SERVICE AND SCOUTING

Looking back, I have realised that (apart from the war) the years in which we grew up, were some of the nicest that I can recall. Today, we have brash noisy discos, but these could never compare to the ballroom dances that we enjoyed towards the end of our school days, and afterwards. Just before leaving school, in the fifth form, we were given a few dancing lessons, which set us on the road to many pleasant evenings afterwards. At that time, really good dances were held in the church halls and in those of the schools, and most weekends there would be a dance at the Winchmore Hill School, or the St. Pauls Institute, or the Royalty Hall, Southgate, and a host of others. There was plenty of choice, the bands were good and the young people could get out and meet others of their own age, in a nice atmosphere.

I remember that it was the girls we got to know, and the dances; which us lads were most reluctant to leave, when we were called up for our National Service, although I feel this did us no harm.

I travelled down overnight to enlist at Bodmin, Cornwall. After six weeks primary training I went to Meanee Barracks, Colchester for ten weeks infantry training – then to Bulford camp on the Salisbury Plain and thence to Mingaladon in Burma. We did not go direct to Burma, but travelled via Singapore, where the draft stayed at Nee Soon transit camp for a few weeks, before travelling by coastal steamer to Rangoon, Burma.

There was a large parade ground at the camp, surrounded by stone built barrack buildings. On this, our first visit, we did not stay in these but were accomodated in a vast tented area on the hills above. There were numerous 'Foxholes' in the sides of the hills, where Japanese soldiers were concealed during the fighting. We had barely got our kit into our respective tents, when I noticed two old Indians come walking down the far end of the road between the tents. We carried on getting organised, and later learned that they were fortune tellers. Two of our soldier friends were most astounded, as each of them had been told the name of his girl friend, their birthday, and the name of the road in which each of them lived. This was in fact the only time that I came across anything of this nature whilst I was abroad in the army.

For most of my time in Burma, I was responsible for the repair and maintenance of the battalion vehicles, until I was sent with the advance party to Egypt, in preparation for the battalion's withdrawal from Burma. I was in Egypt for only a few months before it was time to travel homewards, via Singapore, as my army service drew to a close. Once back in civvy street I enjoyed something of the old life; there were still a certain amount of the dances that I remembered, but most of the old faces had gone. Soon I met my wife (at the Royalty Hall, Southgate), and we settled down, and eventually bought a house in Enfield.

After coming out of the forces I soon became involved in helping to run my old scout troop. On the evening of the day, that we moved into our house in Enfield, I was acting the part of Mae West, in the scout show, being one of the four 'Bold Bad Girls of History', Nell Gwyn was another. Each of us had to sing a solo as we strode forward to the footlights. I was a major success, by treading on the train of my dress, which ripped quite audibly and produced a bout of clapping from the audience. One of the 'Bold Bad Girls', was busily engaged in trying to push two oranges back up 'His' jumper; these seemed determined not to stay in the right place.

For one of my greatest successes, in helping to run the scout troop, I received a reprimand; it happened this way:– Normally, in our troop, it was not possible for two Scouters to be in camp together. Usually one would take the first half, and another would run the camp for the last part. I think it was due to illness, that on this particular occasion, I had sixteen boys to supervise, single handed, for ten days. The camp was located on an estate in a small Northamptonshire village. It was always the understood thing, that when in camp, the troop would attend a morning service in the village church. I decided that it would be best for us to go on the first Sunday that we were in camp, when uniforms would be smart and clean.

As we sat in the pews throughout the service, I realised that the scouts were much impressed to see that this church had virtually an all girl choir. The camp progressed in the usual way for the first few days, and a typical day might start like this:– Reveille would be called at the appropriate time, and then with the boys standing in a circle, the flag would be broken and a short prayer would be said. After this, any particular instruction for the day would be given, and then, I would ask each patrol leader to detail a lad to come to the store tent later, for the day's rations. As each scout came to the stores, I would ask, "Have you washed your hands?" I was most impressed with their honesty, when invariably the answer would be "No", to which I would reply, "Then go and wash them before handling food". The same question would often receive the same answer, from the same scouts, on several consecutive days.

I remember one young scout who seemed very much averse to water. When sent to wash in the morning, it was common to find him not only washing with his duffle coat on and buttoned up, but with the hood turned completely up while he washed his face. I remember that a cold wash all over by the other members of his patrol, cured this habit.

After a few days in camp, I suppose the boys' minds turned to a bit of devilment, and so a young scout – Len Diggins – dared that I would not invite the choir girls to our camp, for an evening. I have always felt that there is some dishonour in not accepting a reasonable dare, and therefore I told him, he was on. I had no idea how this social evening would be achieved, but getting together with the senior scouts, we soon had a plan for the proposed visit. We would have a nice large fire, with plenty of hot embers, and sit around this. We could sing some of the scout songs; and every so often a few of the scouts would act out their sketches, by the light of the fire. While this was going on, other scouts would cook sausages and hand these around together with crusty bread; others would be responsible for cocoa.

The chosen evening arrived and the boys were most pleased to find that **all** the girls came, and were accompanied by the vicar. We had an extremely good evening with never a dull moment, and lots of laughs. It was quite late by the time the activities drew to a close, and the vicar said prayers, and thanked us strangers for a lovely evening. After clearing up, we eventually got to bed.

I believed in running a fairly disciplined camp, in the usual way, but on this occasion I felt that the boys, and indeed I; had earned a lie-in on the following morning.

It seemed like the crack of dawn, on the next day, when an over-zealous and uninformed District Commissioner climbed over the fence to find us all asleep, long after normal reveille time. I gave an explanation, but he did not seem unduly bothered, and did not notify me of his intention to lodge an official complaint. There was at that

A cold morning in a Kent field in 1957, left to right Henry Plastow, Ken Mills and Gerald Plastow, wait while 'Tinkerbell' raises steam.

time a requirement of scout law, that if there is an intention to lodge such a complaint, the Commissioner must notify the Scouter (in charge), before he leaves the site.

The quality of the enjoyment of the previous evening, and that of the return social event given for us in the village hall, to my mind well justified our extra slumber.

On another occasion, I was to supervise the scouts for the first half of a camp. The tents were sent on ahead to arrive at a station near to the camp site. At that time we had five or six senior scouts, who had auto-cycles or lightweight motorbikes. The arrangement was that the senior scouts would go on ahead, by road, on their bikes, and they would make sure the tents and baggage had been delivered to the camp site; then get the tents up, before I arrived with the younger scouts. On arrival, I was surprised to find that there were no tents on the site, and there were no signs of life either. The only discovery I made, was one of the scout's auto-cycle in a nearby barn. We could hear what sounded like the engines of racing cars, in the distance. Later I learned that the senior scouts had arrived as planned, but hearing the racing cars, and knowing a track to be fairly close by, had forgone their duties, and all to a man, had departed to watch the races!

The time was getting on, and it was spitting with rain. I had no idea where the older scouts were, so having full insurance cover, I commandeered the auto-cycle, and made my way to the local railway station, where I discovered the tents were awaiting collection. It did not take long to get these delivered to the site, and then I and the younger boys started to erect them. Before we had finished this, the senior scouts returned. I quickly had them stand in a line, whilst I gave them a thundering good dressing down. The scout who owned the auto-cycle protested strongly.

At the time I thought that something quite unpleasant should be done to them, for their misdemeanours, and told them so, and said that under the same circumstances, I would do exactly the same thing again, as the welfare of the smaller boys must be my first consideration.

Long after we had both left the scouts, the owner of the auto-cycle, Ken Mills, would visit my wife and I, from time to time. I have a very pleasant memory of him giving a wonderful impersonation of myself giving the scouts a dressing down on their return from the races. Of course, we were then **both** men.

Several times over the years, people have asked if I ever wanted sons, but with my experience of boys, gained from the scouts, I have always felt infinitely safer with my three daughters. I learned that boys could be much more mischievous than a wagon load of monkeys!

* * *

The years, after leaving the army, were eventful in other ways. Ordinary people were not terribly well off in those times, and although I had quite a decent job as foreman of a small factory, the cost of travelling fourteen miles each way by road, every day seemed to keep us short, especially as we were involved with buying our own house.

For some while I did the journey on my Norton motor cycle; being very enjoyable in summer, but it could be very cold in winter. Eventually the Norton was sold and we bought an old Morris 8 series 1. This had a badly worn engine, but was otherwise in fairly good order. For some while the Morris did stalwart service, until it had reached the point where it was burning a pint of oil to a gallon of petrol, and oiling up the plugs too frequently, and so something had to be done. The problem was, how could I get to work without the car, and where was the money coming from to buy another engine, at that time? After some thought, the solution seemed to be to find another cylinder block in a breaker's yard, and then I could strip down my own engine, and fit the replacement cylinder block, mainly over a weekend; then there would be little problem with loss of work. (I had previously worked on engine reconditioning, as a motor mechanic, soon after I left the army.)

A friend and I went to a few breakers' yards, and were lucky in finding almost exactly what I needed, close by in Enfield. However, we came to a snag, because this cylinder block was also well worn, and would need reboring. This would be no problem, as there was a firm of reboring specialists in Enfield, but I needed the cylinder block right then so that it could be completed for the weekend, when ample help was available. The breaker was quite willing to reserve the block for me until the weekend, but that would be too late.

It is said that necessity is the mother of invention, and shortage of cash can sharpen the wits! At this time I was not involved with steam models, professionally, although I had made one model engine, with the help of my brother. This I knew was worth a great deal more than the cylinder block; so, the model was taken along to the scrap yard, and offered as security. We were able to come away with the cylinder block, and all was well. At the weekend, when once again I was in funds, we went to pay for the cylinder block, and collect the model engine. The breaker said that he would rather I kept the money, and he kept the model engine.

THERE WAS ANOTHER OCCASION ON WHICH A STRANGE OBJECT WOULD BE USED AS SECURITY.

It was on the evening of the birth of my second daughter, Julie, at Chase Farm Hospital, Enfield. I had driven home from Kilburn, rushed around, changed, and driven off to pick up my mother in order that we could both go and see my wife and the new baby. The visit went well, and after leaving the hospital, I turned left down a steep hill towards Enfield Town. Almost immediately the engine stopped as the car was out of petrol – but no matter, there was a garage part way down the hill, on the left hand side, so we free wheeled into this. With the confidence of a new father, I instructed the attendant – "Fill her up". Unfortunately, he needed paying, and on feeling in my pockets, I discovered that in the rush I had not brought any money with me. This like the petrol had been overlooked.

Ever practical, I realised that the only object I had with me, of value, was my mother; so laughingly I asked the attendant if he would mind if I left her as security, while I went home to get some money, explaining about the new baby. I had noticed that there were a couple of seats in the cubicle by the pumps, and my home was only two miles away. The arrangement worked well, and I was soon back to pay, and collect my mother. However, 'We were not amused', and years later my wife and I ribbed mother regarding her being left as security for a tank-full of petrol! It produced a loud HUMPH. Funds being short in those days, it was not uncommon to run out of petrol. On one occasion, my mother had helped push the Morris a short distance to a garage because of this. No doubt – being left as security for the stuff, was the last straw.

The British Rail Locomotive on which the author rode from Enfield to Liverpool Street.
Photo: R. Swain.

Chapter 5

EYE PROBLEMS, A HEALER AND A HUMOROUS 'SPIRIT'

If it had not been for my eye injuries, I might never have encountered a spiritual healer, or met a medium. As I was just commencing in business; no doubt rather foolishly, I struck a piece of hard metal with a hammer, with the result that it shattered, and a piece of one tenth of an inch in size, passed completely through my right eye, near to the centre. I had the very best of attention, but due to the long period that the eyes were covered, after the injury, they lost the ability to work together. Apart from this, the injury badly affected the vision, also producing a multiple image.

The injury was such that although I could see well with my better eye, there was always another (multiple) image – not so pronounced, but moving about, and not aligning with the vision from my good eye. When examining eyes, which do not have the normal range of vision, it is not uncommon for them to be checked for sensitivity to light. Indeed, I found my problem most demoralising when the light was bright, and the second images were much more pronounced, and bothering. Initially, one of the worst problems was that I often needed to drive at night. When following a vehicle, I saw its two tail lights with the good eye, and quite an array, with the recently injured eye. This eye saw five lights close together, for each of the rear lights of the vehicle in front. Thus for the two lights in front of me I saw twelve lights. In fact any single light, would produce six images.

Although my better eye had suffered a less severe injury, when I was twelve years old, I had been used to pretty good eyesight, and now, I felt somewhat bothered. Whether or not this problem would have diminished, I cannot know, but it had remained unaltered since the injury; probably about a year. However, at this time, I met Roy Swain who lived within a few miles of my home, in Enfield.

Roy first came to see me, because he knew I was involved with steam models, and it transpired that we got to know each other quite well. In fact, some time later, I was allowed to take his beloved 'Violet' to a traction engine rally at Fyfield. She was a Single Crank Compound Burrell Traction Engine of ample proportions, and a will of her own.

On one occasion, I was fortunate in being invited to ride on the footplate with Roy one Saturday evening, when he took his British Railways passenger locomotive from Enfield to Liverpool Street Station on the late run; an experience I enjoyed. It was a lovely sunny evening as we steamed towards London and as we came towards the outskirts, whilst passing over a small bridge, we had a perfect view of the street below, where a young woman (in summer dress) was being escorted by her boy friend. The young man's arm was well around his girl, and on seeing us, he removed this with a flourish and waved us on our way.

I thoroughly enjoyed the rest of the journey to London, where the engine rested for a short while before the return trip. The brass and copper gleamed as it stood silhouetted against the mellow lights of the station. A little smoke from the chimney, and a wisp of steam from an injector drifted off to disappear into the gloom, before the engine was once again steaming back on its return journey to Enfield.

I found the motion of a locomotive much more pleasant than that of the Steam Traction Engines that my brother and I were well used to. We had in fact brought our own engine, a 4 N.H.P. Burrell Tractor 'LION' from Bideford in North Devon via Hatfield to the Woburn Rally in July 1957. This took 4½ days, camping by the roadside as we came. My wife (who was with us) must have been very tolerant, as our first daughter Anne, was at that time only fifteen months old. To quote from my book on the subject of traction engines:– 'That first night the wind coming off the estuary ripped the tent in half, and we awoke to discover the rain falling steadily. This was all part of the toughening up process, and being tired my brother and I wrapped the tent around us and carried on sleeping peacefully. My wife had retreated to the car with our daughter.' Perhaps a somewhat character forming experience. We were involved with another engine 'ISLAND PRINCE' a 4 N.H.P. Burrell Showman's Traction Engine which we helped to bring from the Southampton area to Hatfield, and in late 1957 my brother and I were again busy, bringing a 4 N.H.P. Burrell Tractor 'TINKERBELL' from Horsmonden in Kent to Enfield.

* * *

When I first met Roy he was employed as a fireman on a steam locomotive of British Railways. His regular driver was a Mr. Wesley,

Julie and Linda watch fascinated, as Uncle Gerald shaves at a West Country traction engine rally. Circa 1963.

who happened to be a healer. Roy himself is a believer in the laying on of hands, and therefore, it was not long before he persuaded me to visit Mr. Wesley, to see if anything could be done with regard to my eye problems.

On visiting Mr. Wesley at one of his healing meetings, one could not but be impressed by his sincerity, and that of his fellow healers. There were three chairs positioned in line roughly central in a small room. Those being helped were seated, undergoing the laying on of hands, whilst other people sat around the sides of the room. My first visit was fairly late in the evening, and after I had experienced the healing, it was suggested that I might like to stay behind and have a talk with the healers. We got along very well, and were soon discussing various aspects of healing. I particularly remember a lady healer, who explained to me that a doctor (who had been alive about fifty years earlier), would often be present at the healing meetings, and his sense of humour would make itself known. Naturally this sort of thing was very new to me, and probably I was very sceptical at the time.

At the next healing session, I was able to observe Mr. Wesley go into a form of trance whilst healing, and he spoke in a different voice, as if some other being had taken over from him. This may be rather difficult to accept, and at that time I was neither convinced, nor otherwise. What did impress me immensely was, that when Mr. Wesley was under trance condition, he was able to walk freely about this very crowded room, stepping over peoples' feet, even though his eyes were tight shut.

I went to healing meetings about six times, and on the third occasion, whilst Mr. Wesley was healing myself, he went into trance, and commenced to speak in a different voice. Then a person (in spirit, or Mr. Wesley using a much disguised voice), held a conversation with me, enquiring as to what effect the traffic lights had on my eye problem, and explaining that when he was alive, on earth, there were no traffic lights.

I doubted that I was talking to a person in spirit, at that time, but I can say that after the fourth visit, I no longer had the problem of multiple lights, at night. Indeed, I found that the problems I had experienced were only present, now; when I was very tired. Although it is unlikely that my eyes could ever work properly together again, the difficulties of the second images had become so minimised as to cause me little problem. See footnote.

We cannot know if this state of affairs would have come about, if I had never been to the healer, but it is extremely unlikely, as the condition had been stable for about a year. What I do know, is that if I had not met Mr. Wesley; a wealth of experiences, might never have been enjoyed.

It was the last visit that I made to the healer, with regard to my eye problems. I realised that a big improvement had been brought about, and I did not wish to impose further. Mr. Wesley, in common with most spiritual healers, did not make any charge whatsoever, unless one cared to give a small donation. It is of a certain incident that occurred at this meeting, that I would like to tell. This particular evening, I had already received the laying on of hands, but due to the small size of the room, and the number of people present; it was not really possible to pass around them, and the healers, to get to the door. Therefore I sat down again, in a chair which I had occupied before the healing. Eventually, it was possible for me to make my way to the door, although there was little room, and I needed to step carefully. I had noticed that Mr. Wesley was attending to a patient (who needed more help than usual), and he was in trance. His voice was quite different, and I remember thinking that this must surely be the genuine thing; after all it would require rather good acting, and to what purpose? As I made my way to the door, Mr. Wesley was standing directly behind the last chair, whilst healing. As I attempted to pass him to make for the door, I was clumsy, and tripped over his foot. I immediately said, "I am sorry", and the same 'Trance' voice said, "Oh that is quite all right – it is not my foot". This was absolutely spontaneous, and to this day I believe that I experienced the humour of the doctor (in spirit), that the lady healer had mentioned some time previously.

* * *

It was during the period of my visits to Mr. Wesley, that my mother told me of a young man (who had been in the scouts), being extremely ill with meningitis. It was a Monday when she told me, and said that he was not expected to live. The vicar had offered special prayers for him at the service on the Sunday. The particular evening that I was told, I had arranged to take mother to receive healing help, for arthritis.

I had previously known the power of ABSENT healing, and thus at the end of the visit, I stopped behind to explain to Mr. Wesley the situation with regard to the ex-scout. I clearly remember his instructions. He said, "We will do our best for him", and instructed that wherever we were (mother and I), at ten o'clock that evening, we should stop the car if we had not arrived home, and should concentrate our thoughts on this young man. This we did: I remember pulling the old Morris 8, into the kerb; then we closed our eyes while we concentrated.

It is not important whether one can prove that any help was given, or not. We do know that the vicar had asked for special prayers, and we also know that Mr. Wesley gave his help. However, we learned that this person was taken off the danger list on Tuesday morning, and made a full recovery. I would not attempt to make any claims as to why this apparent miracle cure occurred. We cannot know. What we do know, is that both the vicar and Mr. Wesley were trying to bring about help from God, in whom they both believed, and in whom they put their trust.

During the visits I made to Mr. Wesley, I undoubtedly witnessed immediate cures, especially to those suffering with arthritic problems, of a severe nature. Often, they would go to him, for the first time, doubled up and in great pain, and would be overjoyed and amazed to find that they were able to straighten up, and their affliction was no longer with them. I witnessed the look of amazement, on several occasions, and there could be no doubt that these people had received an immediate cure. What I do not know is whether this was of a permanent nature.

I hope by showing the reader my reactions to these various occurrences, that he or she will realise that my approach to all these matters, is with an open mind.

FOOTNOTE:– As I became much older, the difficulties with my better eye brought about a decision to discontinue driving at night. The injury to this eye was such that the iris has little movement to allow it to restrict bright light, or open to admit poor light. Thus, there are the problems of dazzle, and; being unable to see properly in the darker places, although my vision is normal enough in daylight, therefore it does not worry me unduly. By the time this problem became evident, I had no further need to drive at night (other than for social reasons), so there was no real difficulty. Mentioning this **other** injury is necessary to clarify that the considerable problem of multiple vision did **not** return, **after** the visits to the healer. (Described in this chapter.)

Like many, I feel very fortunate to have enjoyed fairly good eyesight, which many might envy.

Chapter 6

A SAD TIME

It was in the year 1964, just after we had moved to Cambridge, that my young brother Gerald (then 24 years old) was carrying out electrical wiring work for me, when through a most unfortunate set of circumstances, he was electrocuted. At the time, the Electricity Board Inspector reported that all the wiring work was carried out to the proper standards, and he could not fault it; he said that he could easily have suffered the same accident himself, when carrying out wiring work abroad. In fact, without going into details, it was the temporary bridging of the wiring, in order to give me light, which unfortunately killed him. This put live power onto an outside cable, on which my brother was to work on the following morning. Working late, and then the work being interrupted by a night's sleep, were undoubtedly the factors which caused the oversight.

Time is said to be a great healer. Of course, a lot of years have passed and I am able to recount these happenings without the pain, or feeling of terrible loss that I and the family experienced at that time. This was probably the only time I have known, when my wife, and I were quite incapable of doing anything, regardless of the fact that money was short, and one needed to work to live. Our immediate thoughts were that he must be put in the best bedroom. This was one positive act, but little else was achieved, I feel. To experience such a happening must be heart rending at any time, but it seemed to be worse, because this was the depths of winter, and the ground and the lane were covered in snow, and almost impassable.

The local policeman was kindness itself, giving up his day off to give us some much needed company. Finally, funeral directors came to transport my brother to the Chapel of Rest. Because of the conditions, and the difficulties, they came quite late, and I remember the light had gone. The winter had been severe, and it was extremely difficult to stand, let alone carry a coffin, and so it seemed only right, indeed a privilege to help bear my brother's coffin to the hearse.

After some weeks, we forced ourselves back into reality, but there were certain things which we could not get out of our minds. Right from a youngster, I had been fairly close to my brother; indeed, I can remember nursing him to sleep (as a baby), during the war. My wife and I often took him fishing as a young boy, and can remember one humorous occasion when he was fishing, using improvised curtain rods – he cast, and the whole assembly travelled right out into the middle of the river, to float away.

Like most teenagers (at one time), he became somewhat self-centred, and then changed completely and always seemed very keen to help my wife and I, in whatever we happened to be involved.

Eventually, we got back to a normal state of working, and some time went by. However, we both seemed to feel that my brother's death had been one of those things that was meant to be. There is no point in going into details regarding this feeling, other than to say that there were certain things that he had said to us, which were somewhat out of keeping for him, and gave us this impression. Several times, what he said, seemed to be advice for the future, almost as if he knew that he would soon, not be around. See last paragraph of Chapter 7.

After some weeks had passed, we both thought that we would like to pay a visit to Mr. Wesley, to see him once more. There was no particular purpose in this visit other than a friendly one. We were now living in Cambridge, and so we made the journey back to Tottenham. Naturally, he expressed his sympathies at the death of my brother, and then suggested that we might like to visit the Spiritualist Headquarters in Belgrave Square, London. This then, was the introduction to some of the most remarkable occurrences that we have ever experienced. We have only visited the headquarters of this organisation on a very few occasions; at those times, when we had a particular problem, or else when there were two paths to take and we were not sure which one was ours. These visits will be dealt with separately, under their own headings.

Prefix to Chapter 7

INTRODUCTION TO PONIES

Although on moving to the country, we had ideas of having a pony, it was really our daughter Anne who brought this about, by making friends with an old gentleman, with whom the rest of the family soon became firm friends. It seems then that this chapter of our lives, is best described by my daughter, as she remembers it. H.R.P.

When I was about six, I believed that one could make a wish, and provided it remained a secret, it would come true. So, I wished for a pony. I told no-one, and very soon forgot all about it. A year or so went by, and we eventually moved to a small village near Cambridge, to live in a bungalow complete with its own resident cat. It was a lovely place, with a fair sized apple orchard. The front and back gardens were surrounded by plum, cherry plum and greengage trees, and a tall pear tree stood near the front gate. The grass in the orchard had grown so high, that my two sisters and I would play in it for hours and sometimes get lost.

Julie and I went to school in the next village, which meant a three mile cycle ride. Linda my youngest sister, was about three and a half, at the time, and didn't like having to stay at home, so she asked when she would be able to go with us. She was told that she could do so, once she had learned to ride a bike. Needless to say, she learned within a week, and then was told she was not old enough.

It was a nice school, with less than fifty pupils, so you can imagine the hard work and scheming that it took to raise enough money for a swimming pool. The school had to raise £500 and the education authorities then gave a grant for the rest of the money. The headmaster organised several school fetes, and everyone concerned helped to create some form of money making amusement. My father offered to give rides with his model traction engine, as he often did this for charity events.

On the appropriate day, we helped get the traction engine ready, and then set off for school. As the fete opened, I had a wander round. It was then that I saw an elderly man giving rides with his ponies. I asked if I could help lead them up and down the field, and spent most

Anne, Julie and Linda meet a friend on the way home from school. Circa 1966.

of the day doing so. When the fete ended, he very kindly allowed me to ride 'Dot' home, and then offered us girls the chance of riding her at weekends. Julie and I would go to Mr. Ibbott's most weekends after that. He had a long driveway, so there was no need to take 'Dot' out onto the road. She would trot up and down for a while, but would eventually tire of this, and bolt for her field. Once, she threw me into a patch of stinging nettles; being a painful experience, which dented my pride somewhat. Mr. Ibbott was a lovely man, very down to earth and hard working, and when we first knew him, he had not long sold his garage business at Sutton, Cambs.

After some time, my parents realised that we enjoyed riding enough to have our own pony, and were prepared to do our share of the work in looking after one. So, one day my long forgotten wish came true. We went to a common in Cambridge to buy a Welsh Mountain pony; a lovely chestnut gelding, called Ben. He soon settled down and it was not too long before we bought a bay mare called Jane, to keep him company.

I have often thought that the lot of a horse may not be an enviable one, sometimes, after purchase they may not jump high enough, or move fast enough, despite perhaps the limited ability of the rider, and are sold on. It must be very unsettling. I remember the family went on holiday in a boat on the River Cam, one year, and we left the two ponies on a meadow belonging to dad's friend Mr. Howe. He was kind to animals, and had owned horses himself, for many years. On going to the meadow to collect the ponies on returning from our holiday, Ben was so excited at finding that he hadn't been sold, that he tore round and round the field, until he slipped sideways on the lush grass, and pulled a muscle in his shoulder.

As time went by Mr. Ibbott became ill. His sister looked after him for a while, until eventually he went to live with her. Gradually he returned to his former self and would once again potter around the garden. In the summer, he would cut and turn the grass, with his little tractor, making hay for our horses. When this was ready he would phone, so that we could collect; he would not take a penny for it.

Mr. Ibbott encouraged the local children to ride, and this undoubtedly gave lasting pleasure to them, as it did to my sisters and I.

A.C.E.

Chapter 7

A FIRST VISIT TO A MEDIUM, A BOAT IN SAFE HANDS AND A PONY CALLED 'BEN'

Before moving to Cambridge, I had been building an 18-foot cabin cruiser; in the back garden. My brother, a senior scout, often took or helped to take parties of scouts on the River Thames, by canoe. He was well familiar with the river and enjoyed being on the water with the boys, and camping on the river bank at night. His experience would have been invaluable with the boat, and we expected to use it together when it was completed. By the time that we moved to Cambridge, the hull was completely finished and the fore-deck was being fitted.

We hired a mobile crane to lift the boat out of the garden and onto the lorry for transporting to Cambridge and once there, the boat was off loaded and chocked, and supported into position, and covered with tarpaulins. Naturally, with the accident that transpired (Chapter 5), the boat received no further attention.

The reader will recall that Mr. Wesley had suggested a visit to the

The boat, some time after being sold, and fully completed. Photo: by courtesy of the owner.

Spiritualist Association of Great Britain, headquarters, London. Eventually, we made an appointment by phone. Now, it seemed to us that if a medium was genuine, we could simply arrive at the correct time, and meet the medium, without making any request, or asking any questions. Quite apart from this being prompted by any scepticism, it seemed to be the right thing to do, to let any information come freely from those in the spirit world, without blocking their efforts, by one's requests. We paid a very reasonable fee for the sitting, and then went upstairs to a small room where we met a medium, Kathleen St. George. We were in a small bright room with the sunlight coming through the window, and the roar of London's traffic below. It was certainly not the sort of setting one might imagine.

We found this lady to be a very gifted medium. After a prayer and without a word from ourselves (apart from initial greetings), she started to describe the persons (in spirit) around us who were making themselves available. By the descriptions, one could be in little doubt that the medium was absolutely genuine. For my wife's father, she described a man holding out his right hand to show that it was drawn up like someone with arthritis, but that it was not arthritis. In fact, he had fallen on a milk bottle as a child, and the glass had badly cut the leaders, causing this deformity. For my wife's grandfather, a tall military looking man standing on top of a cliff – a very good description, and the cliff identified him, because he was very fond of Westcliffe on Sea and went there for his holidays, for many years. My brother then came to the forefront, and the medium said that he had been killed, and he was telling us that it was not his fault. I had never really thought about this, until this moment of writing, and realise that he certainly would not have considered that it was my fault either; and so, maybe it **was** one of those things that were meant to be.

Now, to the most impressive part of our visit! The medium suddenly said, "You are expanding" – I replied, "**No** I am **not** expanding", and as is the way with mediums (who are very sure of their facts), she said, "You are definitely expanding", to which I replied, "**No** I am **not**". She said, "I am being shown a building that is only partly erected, putting up a building is expanding". She carried on to say, "Your brother says that you must get on and finish it". I agreed that she was perfectly correct. In fact my brother was to have helped me put this building up, for a workshop.

There were many other pieces of information passed on at this time, including telling me that I could divine – did I know? (See relevant chapter.) But the most impressive piece of information was the last. Suddenly she said, "You have a boat" – to which I replied that I had. She then told us that my brother was holding up a tin of **what looked like paint**, but in fact **was not**; and she said that he is telling you that there is nothing wrong with the boat at the moment, but if you do not do something about it straightaway, there soon will be!

Various other persons were mentioned at this sitting, and each and every one could easily be identified, apart from the name of one young man, which meant nothing to us. Strangely enough, this same name was mentioned again on another occasion, but we were unable to identify its owner. It could easily have been the name of someone with whom my brother was friendly, but we did not know ourselves.

We will return to the boat:– With such positive information given to us, with regard to this, it was easy to check the validity of the advice on the following day. On lifting the tarpaulin from the boat, it was found to have leaked, and there was roughly six inches of water in the bottom. Yet, exactly as my brother had imparted through the medium; there was nothing wrong with it at that moment – in fact the wood had not commenced to rot. The water was duly baled out, after which the boat was allowed to thoroughly dry out, and then, as per the medium's interpretation, it was treated with something that **looked like paint, but was not** – rot proofing liquid.

We are now moving towards a period in our lives when we were to have experiences which would defy all normal explanation, and which we consider ourselves very privileged to have been involved in. Although, definitely not members of any spiritualist church, or organisation, and not being practising members of any particular religion, we had purchased two books from the Spiritualist Headquarters. One concerned healing, and another, on mediumship. From these I learned of some of the beliefs of the Spiritualist Church, and tried putting a few into practice.

Following the accident, we lost interest in the boat. This was about three quarters built, and one would have thought to be 'A good buy', but it seemed most difficult to sell. It was well made, and of good materials, but we did not seem to get any response to our adverts. We felt that we had no further use for the boat, especially as we had intended using it with my brother. Thus, it seemed that there was no further interest in the boat, and therefore it should be disposed of. This then was the frame of mind we were in when we were advertising it. Eventually, after reading theories of positive thinking, in one of the booklets, we decided that it was high time that we bought our girls a pony. After all, we had intended doing this, but the unfortunate accident had pushed this from our minds. We made a positive decision, the boat must be sold, and this would finance the purchase of a pony. Within a few days, not only had we sold the boat, but we had found the perfect pony. He was called Ben, being a twelve hand Welsh Mountain pony – very loveable but with a quite fiery temperament at times. We were fortunate in having him with us for sixteen years, until 1981, when at 21 years old, he became very ill and had to be put down.

I hope my readers will understand that every day happenings have been very much interwoven with those of a more extraordinary nature throughout our lives. The next part of this account of strange happenings, is very closely connected with 'Ben'.

In the early days, we were quite green with regard to the keeping and riding of horses, but had always been practical people, also luckily we had a fair amount of grassland. Seeing an advert in the paper, we went along to see 'Ben'. Looking back we were very fortunate, because we really knew very little about horses, and yet that afternoon, we bought the most perfectly made animal that one could wish for. Wherever he went, he was admired, and several people almost begged us to sell him to them. However, it has always been our practice to keep our horses right throughout their lives, and therefore he was never sold.

We decided to enlist the aid of the local riding establishment, and so, we arranged that Ben would be taken from our home (by one of the stable girls), and then our daughters would go over to Bourne at a weekend, and ride him, groom him and get thoroughly used to him. At the same time we would go along and improve our knowledge. Ben was duly collected on the Friday evening, and the girl rode him through the bridle paths, a matter of about four miles, to the stables. Our girls spent most of the weekend there, after which we brought them back home, in our van. Later the girl would ride Ben back to us.

Our living room was on the back of the bungalow, opening up to a path and garden by full length metal framed glass doors. While waiting for Ben's return, we took the opportunity to have some tea.

We well remember the sight of Ben appearing at the door on his return. It was dark, but the light shone out, as the doors were not curtained. The girl advised us to put a blanket on him because it was cold, and he was warm from the journey. After making him comfortable in his stable, my eldest daughter Anne and I, took the stable girl back to the riding centre, at Bourne.

Naturally, we were all excited about the purchase of Ben and on the return journey, Anne and I were talking about the pony, and she said that Uncle Gerald (my brother), would be pleased about Ben.

Anne and Ben. 1967.

As near as we can tell, at the same time when we were thinking of my brother and saying that he would be pleased, a voice was heard outside of the French windows of our bungalow. At this time, Anne and I would have been almost to Bourne. The voice was heard by my wife, and the two younger daughters, and this was the voice of my brother, who said, "Alright Anne?" This voice was so plain, that although it was exactly as the voice of my brother, my wife thought that the only explanation could be that Anne and I had come back, for some reason or other. My brother's voice was somewhat similar to mine, so this must be the answer. In fact, when my wife opened the door there was no-one there.

I firmly believe that they experienced the not uncommon phenomenon of direct voice contact, by a person in spirit, at a time when sufficient thought in the right direction, made this possible. In no way would my wife and daughters have expected our return, so soon; nor would they have expected anyone else either, at night; as we lived in a fairly isolated location.

We accepted and were pleased by this contact from my brother; but, there were to be two more from him. These contacts were such that two of them involved more than one person, making them very difficult to disprove. In one instance he showed concern for myself, which was typical of his nature before he had the accident.

* * *

On one occasion when my wife and I went to a medium, she said that my brother was holding an object which was similar to a camera, but could not tell what it was. She said that the message he was giving, was that he would prove life after death. I do not believe we have ever expected some miracle sign in conjunction with an object looking somewhat like a camera; but will describe an event which involved an object about the same size and appearance as a camera.

Some months after my brother's death, my sister and her husband visited us at Cambridge, and we got to talking about our brother. My wife and I expressed the opinion that his death was one of those things that was meant to be. No doubt my sister was still very upset, and emphatically denied the possibility. Immediately, as she spoke, all the lights went out, and we heard the click of the trip switch. My first thought was that there must be a short circuit on the outside cables, but on checking, I remembered that the cable which fed **all** the outbuildings was still disconnected from the time of the accident. Country properties, with overhead power supply are generally fitted with a trip switch. These operate, or trip out, if a short circuit occurs. On pressing the switch back up into place, the lights all came back on, and there was found to be **no fault** to the system whatsoever. The trip switch was black, about the same size as a camera, and could easily be taken for one!

Chapter 8

DIRECT VOICE CONTACT WHILE MOWING

It was a particularly busy time; building up a business, and getting our new home organised, made for long days, and one often felt very tired. Our land was always very wet, because apart from being heavy soil, it had a layer of clay about a foot beneath the surface, and thus very little drainage took place. From our orchard, the water would make its way down, to the area of the front garden, and the lawn became very soft and difficult to keep cut. I remember very well, just as if it had happened only yesterday. I had been working late, and went straight on to cut the front lawn, as I felt that if I did not, with the rain that was imminent, it might well be impossible for some time.

At that time we had a simple hand propelled rotary mower, very effective but hard going on soft ground. I was obviously in a perfectly receptive state of mind, no doubt because of being rather tired, and just propelling the mower in ever decreasing circles to get the job done, and this needing no particular thought. The mower was driven by a petrol engine and was quite noisy. Suddenly, the unmistakable voice of my brother almost shouted at me – "Your tea's ready!!" If it was possible, I might have jumped out of my skin. This was loud, unmistakable, and heard completely above the sound of the mower. The message was clear – you have done enough!

I am quite sure that persons in a higher existence (in spirit form), can communicate, when conditions are right; both by actual sound and also by projecting the sound, which may then be heard only by the person for whom it is intended. Normally the ears pick up sound waves, which pass a message to the brain and thus the sound registers with us. The same thing happens with the senses of sight, touch and smell. I believe that it is perfectly possible for sound communication to come from a person in spirit, by a contact being made with the sound receiving section of the brain; direct. We must realise that when one is in the presence of a medium, all manner of unshakeable messages will come through, and yet no-one other than the medium is aware of them.

Direct contact with the brain to impart sound, would appear to be much more likely in some instances than others. The mower was quite noisy, and yet the message "Your tea's ready" seemed to predominate over all other sound. I remember looking all around me to see where the person was, who shouted. But, there was no-one there.

Chapter 9

A PROOF OF LIFE AFTER DEATH?

Perhaps a year went by after our first visit to the medium in London, and we were busy with the business, and made several friends. We had purchased a second horse Jane, a 15 hh. bay mare, and did a fair amount of riding, although for some while, this was mainly by Anne, my wife and myself, as the other two girls were still rather young. Looking back, this period was the commencement of one of the most pleasant in our lives. There were many very lovely bridle paths and green lanes in the Cambridge area, and the landowners seemed to be keen to help preserve them.

After some time, we got around to thinking that we might like to make another visit to the S.A.G.B. in London, and see the same lady medium. The thought had occurred to us on several occasions, until we made a definite decision, and phoned and made an appointment. Now, I would ask the reader to study in great detail what I am about to relate, as if not absolute proof of life after death, then it must be about the nearest thing possible.

We had arranged to see the medium about the middle of the next week. Strangely enough, one evening, I received a phone call from my old friend and workmate, Eric Crowe, who I had worked with in tool making. I had not seen Eric for quite a long while, probably about eighteen months. On this particular evening, when he phoned, he asked to speak to me, and then enquired, "How are you, are you all right?" Eric normally had no difficulty in talking, in fact, just the reverse, but during this particular phone call, I felt that here was a man who had been directed to contact me, and yet now, did not know what to say. Very little was said on this occasion.

The reader will remember that my wife and I had an appointment with the medium, during the following week. Once in her presence, we had barely sat down when this good lady stated:– "You have a friend called Eric" to which I replied, "Yes I have." Her exact words were – "Well, he may know, or he may not know, but your brother has been trying to contact him."

I would like to say a little about my old friend Eric. I worked with him at the toolmakers in Waltham Abbey for perhaps a year or so. We got on very well together, and Eric gave me the impression of being very perceptive. However, some of the happenings that he related, concerning himself or his family, really did take quite a bit of believing, even for a person such as myself. I will recall just two of the occurrences that he described to me. Eric told me that when one of his sisters was at home, there were often strange happenings. One evening he said that there had been disturbances in the house, which could not be accounted for, and he and his sisters were so bothered by these, that eventually they all went into a bedroom at the top of the stairs, to give them moral support. He said that shortly there were heavy footfalls on the stairs, coming up towards the bedroom; he was so scared, that he picked up the poker (went halfway down the stairs) and swung this at whatever was there; although, there was nothing to be seen. Once he returned to the bedroom, the heavy footfalls continued from where they had left off and completed their journey to the top of the stairs. This incident occurred before he was married, and a later one happened when I worked with him. He came in to work one morning, and immediately told me about it. He said that he had been sitting in the kitchen, the previous evening, when a bottle of milk that was on the fridge, had suddenly tipped over on its side. It lay horizontal, while the milk poured out, and then, as if this was not sufficient, the bottle had up-ended to empty out the last few drains. Who in their normal senses would believe such tales; and yet, I have no doubt now, that Eric was telling the absolute truth.

The reader will recall that Eric had phoned just two or three days before our visit to the medium, when she stated that my brother had been trying to contact him. Naturally, when I returned home, the first thing I did was to phone him. He said that he would like to come down to see us, and did so on the following Sunday.

What Eric told us, was quite remarkable. I knew that he had a Dobermann Pinscher dog, which was typical of its breed. Eric would often take the dog on the Cheshunt Marshes for a walk, and he said that on several occasions, when walking completely alone, other than with the dog; a voice had called – "Eric" – being loud and distinct and drawn out, and sounded like it came from some little way off. He explained that when this happened, the dog would cringe at his feet; something he had never seen it do before. He said that he looked behind the bushes, but there was no-one there. He carried on to explain, that every time the voice called, he saw my face, quite plainly, and thus, his immediate thoughts were that I was in trouble. This then was why he had phoned me.

I think the reader will agree that this series of occurrences, must be close to proving life after death. There are in fact, four people involved, because my wife was present with the medium, in London; Eric Crowe, who I had not seen for about eighteen months; the medium Kathleen St. George, and my brother, in spirit. We have absolutely no fear of being contradicted with regard to these incidents.

Through all the important occurrences, concerning spiritual manifestation, that I and my family have observed; there is one remarkable, and I am sure **intentional** feature. That is the **timing**! Consider that Eric was contacted by my brother, at the perfect opportune time, when my wife and I had arranged to see the medium. She in her turn was able to complete the contact, only because the timing was right. This same timing makes itself evident in several of the occurrences. In the case of 'The Little Old Lady', she is witnessed on four occasions, by different people at different times, and yet, these people all know each other, and all just happen to mention the apparition, at the right time to corroborate the matter.

Chapter 10

THE POWER OF ABSENT HEALING, AND HELP FROM FRIENDS ABOVE

Time passed, the younger girls were now riding the pony, and I suppose we had got down to a routine in our country life. One day, our middle daughter Julie, (then about eight years old), became ill. It started with her being sick and then it became quite impossible for her to keep any food or drink down. This went on for several days, until the doctor decided to have her taken to hospital. We visited her there for three days, and each time we could see that she was deteriorating fast. She could not keep anything down, not even water. We were very worried, and said to the nurse in charge, that surely she must soon start dehydrating; and were told that she had not started yet. But, still the hospital were unable to discover what was wrong with her. My wife and I were very concerned because Julie just laid there with no interest in anything, or anybody.

We came out of the hospital, extremely worried, and decided that we should contact the healer, Mr. Wesley to see if he could help her. Immediately outside the hospital was a phone box, therefore I made a call, and was very fortunate in getting straight through to him. I explained how ill Julie was, and the fact that the hospital had not discovered what was wrong with her. I had barely finished my explanation, when Mr. Wesley said "She has a blockage in the stomach." He said that he would do what he could for her, and we thanked him.

When we had left Julie, in the ward, there had been a lady visiting her daughter, in a bed adjacent to Julie's. She had stayed behind, after we had left. (Visiting for the children was more or less at any time.)

The following day, we went in to see Julie, and were amazed to see her sitting up, and looking bright and cheerful, and giving the impression of being in the best of health. The lady mentioned, told us that she had never seen anything so remarkable in her life. She said that almost immediately after we had left the ward, (in fact just about exactly the time that I was speaking to Mr. Wesley), Julie had suddenly sat up in bed, combed her hair and then watched television, and asked for a drink. The improvement was so remarkable, that we were allowed to take her home that afternoon, and she had no further trouble.

We feel that it must be some sort of tragedy, that people such as ourselves, who have experienced healing, should need to be desperate before seeking the good help of a spiritual healer.

Several examples of healing are described in this book. This is not an indication that it will ALWAYS bring an immediate cure, it will not, but in those cases where help is possible, I think it very likely that the belief and trust of those persons seeking help, may go a long way to making conditions suitable for healing to work.

* * *

Life seemed to go fairly smoothly through the next couple of years, and I think my belief in life after death, and the world of those in spirit, must have become pretty absolute.

There are certain happenings, which without the back up of other experiences, one might discard as being coincidence. For the first period that I was in business, I carried out sub-contract work, and for this I would often make jigs and fixtures, since orders would often be repeated. I accumulated a lot of these pieces of equipment, and naturally, one could not always find the particular one that was required, as it may have been a year since it was last used. Often, I would think to myself – now where is that tool; and try as I might, I would not be able to find it. However, after I had run out of places to look, my mind would often go blank, and then I would find myself taking three or four steps, or walking round behind a bench, and would become aware that I was looking directly at the tool that was required. This particular occurrence has long been something I accept as help, and when this happens I always say "Thank you". Such occurrences can be coincidence for once, twice or even six times, but after this I feel there should be some sort of acceptance. Perhaps this occurrence is akin to divining, Chapter 21.

The reader will recall that I advocate acceptance of the spirit world, in order to advance in knowledge, and to receive help. I believe, that one must look on our friends in spirit, in the same way as we would think of our workmates, associates, or friends and family. Indeed, did dying make some of them any less dear, or related to us?

Make them feel wanted, and accepted. I think I must have achieved some sort of compatibility, with those in the spirit world, as on one occasion, I referred to them as "You buggers" – and the help was immediately given. I trust I may not offend some of my readers, but this is a true account, and it is also about life as it is lived.

I have never subscribed to the idea that persons who swear occasionally; only do this because of their inability to express themselves. I would term this as snobbish poppycock! Whereas, I cannot tolerate some of the filthy language that is used on the television these days; I have never thought a few minor swear words did any harm. Indeed, they can do an awful lot of good. Can one imagine a workman striking his finger with a hammer, and saying "Dash it old boy", when a few good expletives go so very much further in helping to relieve the pain, whilst he is still dancing in agony.

A Mr. Read, in Cambridge where I lived often did welding work for me, and on one particular occasion he asked if I could oblige, and do a job for him. I was given the work early in the week and told that there was no rush, until the Thursday evening, or Friday. Now to carry out this job, I needed to use my three (engineers) 'G' clamps, to hold the work for me. It was the beginning of the week, and the job was a small one, so I did not intend to start it straightaway. However, I came to realise that I had not seen my 'G' clamps recently, and so kept them in mind as I moved about the foundry, and workshop. It got to about Thursday mid-day, and I still had not found these wretched clamps, and now of course the job needed to be done. Once again I looked around, with no luck.

I thought of my friends in the spirit world, and after leaning against my big old lathe and shutting my eyes, I said aloud "Come on you buggers, where are my G clamps?" Immediately into my mind came two words – LAMP BRACKET. I knew that mediums often receive approximate descriptions, when receiving messages, and so I walked around the workshop, and said aloud – "Now what could I conceivably call a lamp bracket, in here?" Seeing nothing to fit the description, I went into the foundry building; I saw a red pig lamp hanging from a large circular mould box, which in turn was hanging on a nail on the wall. Immediately below this were three piles of mould boxes, stacked to form a 'U' section, on the bench. The bench they rested on was in fact only about eighteen inches high, and was used to put moulds on while we poured molten metal into them. The

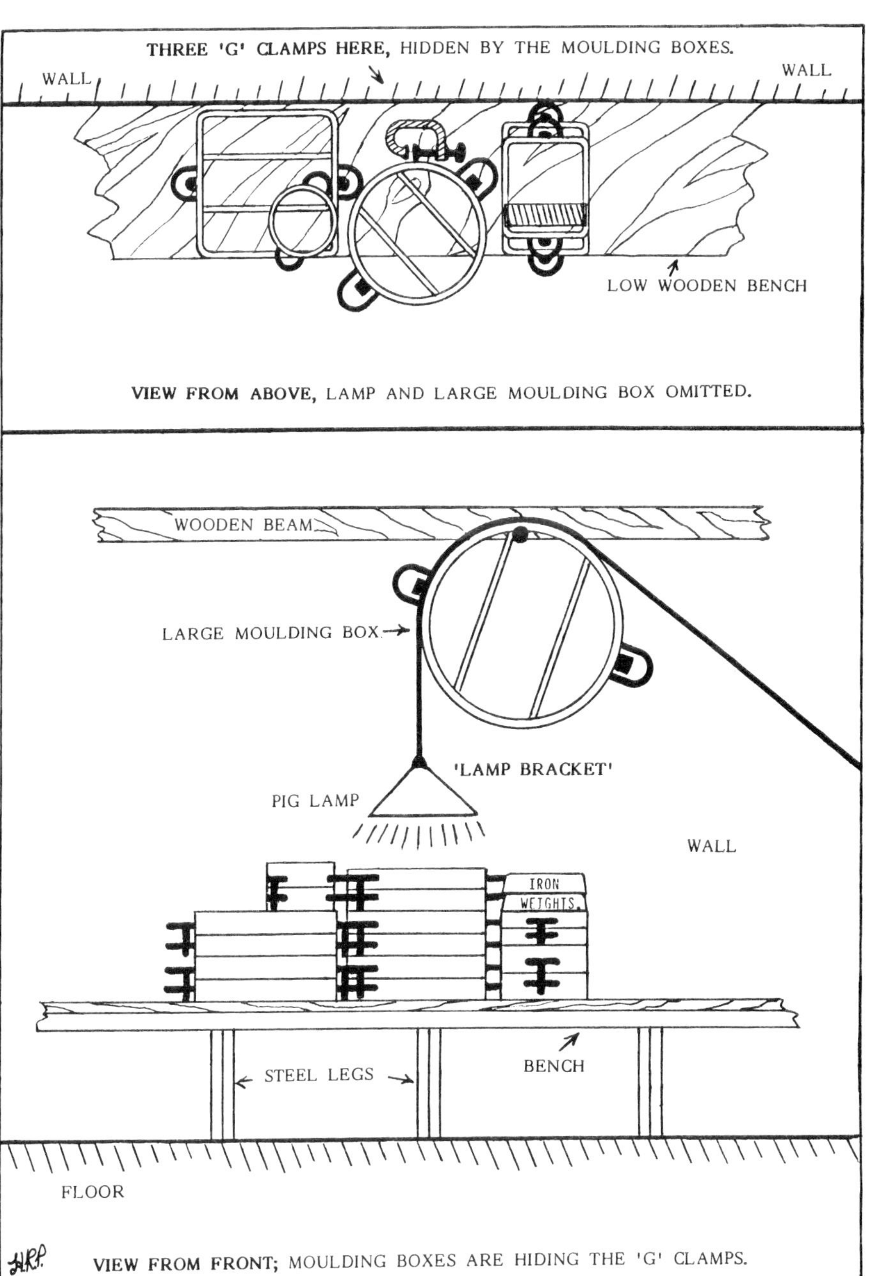

The 'Lamp bracket', and moulding boxes.

pig lamp was used to illuminate the mould boxes, in order to see the feed holes in the sand, so that we could direct the flow of metal down these.

On looking at the pig lamp, with its shade, hanging on the mould box – I thought – yes one could describe that as a lamp bracket, and on looking immediately below the lamp, there were my 'G' clamps, on the bench, and completely hidden by the three stacks of mould boxes. See illustration.

Until writing with regard to the 'G' clamps, the significance of my using mild blasphemy had not occurred to me. On reflection, I realise that there are two forms that swearing would normally take. One is the use of such words when tempers are raised, and the other can more or less be described as a form of endearment. One might refer to their friends or workmates as "You buggers", after some mild prank, but it would be used in a friendly spirit. Is it possible that by the use of mild blasphemy – that in fact, I was treating those persons in the next life, exactly in the same way as I would my friends, or the persons that I might work with. Thus instead of being all serious, and making a formal request for help in finding my clamps, I made an urgent request in a more relaxed, and friendly way, making communication easier.

Chapter 11

SEEING INTO THE FUTURE, AND 'OLD NICK'

We lived in Cambridge for eight very pleasant years, until a large development scheme overtook the area, and we ultimately moved to Suffolk. However, there were various other happenings before we finally left, but I would like to relate two, which are different.

The reader will recall that we had purchased a book on healing, and another on mediumship. It was not with any intention of becoming seriously involved with either practice, although on more than one occasion, my wife and I had been told that we could both heal, and become mediums. I will deal with the small amount of healing in which I became involved; in another chapter.

On one occasion, after reading the booklet on mediumship, I decided to carry out the initial procedures that were recommended. I can recall that the booklet advised that any attempt at contact with the spirit world; should be made in the company of another person. What I did then (and have occasionally tried since), was to think of something beautiful, like a cock pheasant, strutting in the field. One concentrates on a mental picture, being aware of the various colours, mannerisms etc., until he becomes real in the mind, and the more one concentrates, the more complete the picture becomes. Subconsciously, the grass waves in the breeze, one hears the hum of insects, and perhaps a bird flies by.

Another method I remember, was to imagine you are walking down a long avenue of trees, moving towards the light, at the end. This can create the same effect. After a while, with the mind clear of all other thoughts, the picture will fade, and then it may well be replaced with something of significance to the medium.

My wife and I have rarely sought spiritual contact other than by our few consultations with a medium. However, the possibilities were made plain to me one evening. I had gone through the preliminaries, when the mental picture of **my** making; was replaced. I could see inside a church, in fact I was viewing the scene, from the right hand side of a coffin. I could see the altar, with the candles lit, all of the details of the altar-end of the church were plain to see. At the same time as I received this picture I was made aware that this was a funeral that I would hear about, and yet it would cause me **no** grief. Such then must be the manner in which mediums receive their information. What I marvelled at, was the completeness of the message that was given to me. It was not told in words, but was imparted in its entirety, instantly to the mind, without any form of sound being used.

I will not give details of what I learned on the following day, as this could cause upset. However, I did see very accurately into the future, and this was corroborated on the very next day, when a tradesman, delivering to us, told of a fatal accident that had occurred to a friend of his on the previous day.

* * *

When one uses genuine mediums, it is often quite surprising how sure they are of their facts, even to the point of contradicting the person sitting with them. See Chapter 7.

On one occasion I had a man working for me on the Streatham Beam Engine. We had been involved with model steam engines, for years, and at this time he was making sketches of the various parts of this steam engine, in order that we could produce working drawings, and patterns from them.

During the period that this work was being carried out, two Americans happened to visit the Streatham Beam Engine, and saw the engineer carrying out the dimensional sketches, and later wrote to us, to enquire about our range of models. The writer said that he was most impressed with the care that was being taken in copying down the details, although the letter did not mention the particular component that was being drawn at the time of the visit.

Some days later, the young man and I, were working together on the sketches, and going through them, in order that I would fully understand them. I happened to mention to him the compliment that had been passed, with regard to his care, and showed him the letter. He said "Let me see, what was I drawing at the time they were there?" – To which I replied, "A main crank bearing" – he almost jumped out of his chair with surprise, and demanded "How did you know?" – I said "I did not know **how** I knew, but I **did** know."

Purposely, I have not mentioned the name of the young man, as at the time, he seemed somewhat bothered. Perhaps he thought that I was 'Old Nick', or maybe that I had been spying on him.

These then are two instances which show that it is possible to see into the future, and sometimes to obtain information, that is not available in the normal way.

Jane, in 1983. An old lady.

Chapter 12

COUNTRY LIFE

Hordes of chattering Fieldfares would descend on our orchard each year, to herald the snow, and the real winter weather. Going up the field one bitter day to bring the horses into the stable, we were delighted to see a large 'V' formation of geese fly low over the trees. As the snowflakes drifted down, the geese honked their way across the orchard to disappear into the gloom. The countryside offers many such compensations for its bleak weather.

By now, all the family had become well used to horses. In fact, more or less by necessity, I had learned to shoe our own horses, as we found it often difficult to obtain the services of a blacksmith; a dying breed in the area at that time. The man who taught me to shoe, had been in the German Cavalry in the last war, and had a narrow escape, when a horse was shot from under him when crossing the Russian lines. Hans told us that in the German Cavalry, all troopers had to be able to shoe their own horses. He taught me the Continental method of shoeing, whereby one person holds up the foot, whilst another carries out the work. Hans became a prisoner of war and was brought to England, where he married and settled down, living locally to us when we first met him.

When we first bought Jane, our mare, her feet were in a quite dreadful state, probably due to poor feeding before the riding stable had purchased her. The hooves were so brittle that for the first few months, shoeing was something of a problem, until good food and care rectified this. Today, at twenty seven years old, she has as fine a set of hooves as any horse could wish for, tough and hard wearing, and never needing to be shod, because she is rarely ridden. I have mentioned Jane, because it is often said that animals are particularly receptive to thought, personality and to supernatural occurrences. Regarding the first, when riding Jane I often used to feel that she could read my mind. A simple example of this happened when I was riding back through the village of Toft one day, and taking a lane that wound behind the village. I came to School Lane on my left, which I did not normally use. Momentarily I thought to myself – I'll go through here today for a change, but in fact changed my mind almost instantly. However, although I gave no signal to the horse, Jane abruptly turned left as the first thought crossed my mind. Just another example of E.S.P. Anyone who knows horses will be aware that a horse turned towards home is keen to go by the shortest route, and one that it knows, not turning readily onto a different track.

A horse will also react to temperament. It was always very noticeable, that the minute I got into the saddle, she would be off, giving of her best and then being difficult for other people to ride. Conversely, when my wife rode Jane, she would be much quieter, and more manageable. Of the perceptiveness of animals to the supernatural, I shall refer later.

We were happy in Cambridge, and had some good times with the horses. The county in general was very nice, there being lots of green roads and bridleways, and to a very large degree, the countryside was unspoiled. Greed has taken so much of our National Heritage in some other parts of the country.

During one summer, two French girls came to stay with us for three weeks, being part of a school exchange visit. Ben somehow managed to get out of his paddock, and was first noticed when one of the French girls happened to look out of the window. Her sudden loud exclamation of "It is hee-e" was one of the few times she plucked up courage to speak any English.

The locality where we lived was very definitely not scheduled for development, and had been under the control of the Cambridge Colleges in the past. However, the persistent endeavours of one man involved the whole area in a large building scheme, and the former way of life was gone for ever. It was time to move on.

Chapter 13

DECIDING ON A NEW HOME, WITH THE HELP OF A MEDIUM

Looking for a new home can be a slow business, and one may be uncertain in their decision. We viewed various properties, one of which was an Old Rectory in Suffolk. In fact, we looked over this property on more than one occasion, because although we liked it, and there was a reasonable amount of grassland for the horses; the house was larger than we had intended purchasing. There was something about this property which seemed right to us, on the other hand there would be a fair amount of maintenance. Being keen on wildlife, the copses and the shrubberies were ideal, although at the time we viewed on the first occasion; the pond located in some old church ruins as a Victorian folly, seemed anything but welcoming. It was raining, the wind blowing, and was very miserable cold and overcast.

We liked the house, which seemed to have a friendly atmosphere, but because of its size, and some other considerations, we were definitely uncertain; in fact we came back several times. When there are two roads to take, one can seek advice or make up one's own mind. We all felt that there could be a lot going for this property, but were still unsure, and therefore we contacted the S.A.G.B. London. Once again, we saw the medium Kathleen St. George, without making any comment, or explaining why we were there.

Undoubtedly there are persons who are gifted mediums, who have exploited their abilities for maximum profit and sensationalism. These perhaps, gifted people have sometimes, in the past brought disrepute on genuine and dedicated mediums.

From the few visits that we had already made to the medium, it will be obvious that we had received a wonderful amount of help, and let alone this, there can be little doubt that the reasonable fee that we had paid, was an extremely good investment. Consider for one moment, that but for the advice with regard to the boat, and the water that had leaked into it; the boat could have been scrap, if the lower section of the hull had been allowed to rot.

Because of our previous experiences with this lady medium, and the accuracy of the information received, we must have gone to her with trust, and very little doubt. After the usual prayer in a perfectly bright room, almost immediately, she said "Does Suffolk mean anything to you?" To this I replied "Yes there is a property in Suffolk that we are considering buying." She said "This is your place." She then went on to describe the property, saying that there was a gravel drive leading up to the house, and then a long gravel path leading up to a church at the top of the property. In fact, there are the church ruins, already mentioned. She asked if we minded what she said to us, and then said that the property was haunted. We had already commented on the thoroughly relaxed atmosphere inside the house, and did not feel there was anything unpleasant at the Old Rectory. Another piece of information imparted, was that there was an asparagus bed at the property, of which we were unaware at that time. The accuracy and extent of the information and description of the property was such as to amaze us. I believe **all** doubts must have been removed, and this, allowed free contact to take place with those in spirit. The medium imparted that a Rector, who had lived in the property, knew that we (my wife and I), were interested in healing. He told us that in his time (on earth), he had practised healing, and this was not just the healing of the sick. It was also the giving of advice, or a little money, or help in various ways. (This contact came through the medium, and not direct.) The medium said again that this was very definitely our place, although she knew that the size of the house had made us uncertain. The property **was** large, and there would be a great deal of work in getting it organised, but we must take our time, and providing we did this, we would find that everything would work out exactly as we would wish. We had no further doubts with regard to the purchase, and in fact, exactly as predicted the move and the settling in went steadily, without any problems. (After living here now for a number of years, we can say that the choice was a wise one.) The statement that the house was haunted, was quite correct as the reader will realise, as my account progresses.

The lane past the Rectory to the church carries on through cultivated land, and as one nears the top of the road, it turns left immediately after a pond, and continues to and alongside the church. This lane was more grand years ago, being a favourite walk of the local people. In those days, there was a wide tree lined avenue (flanked by hedges), for the full length of the Rectory property. At the time of writing, there is a man in the village who remembers (as a boy), being paid 6d each Sunday, to watch over two carriage horses while the service was in progress. It would have been pleasant and relaxing to have ridden to church in a trap; one can imagine the strains of the organ being accompanied by the jingle of harness, as the horses cropped the grass in the lane on a bright summer's evening. These were elegant times and one can visualise a similar scene when the ladies came by trap to play tennis or croquet on the Rectory lawn.

On our first visit to the church we had quite a surprise; on passing through the gate to the churchyard, just on the left, we saw a fine stone monument to the sister of the second incumbent to reside at the Old Rectory. It was the christian names which caught our eye – Juliet Anne, since my middle daughter is called Julie, and my eldest daughter is called Anne. Certainly strange, perhaps only coincidence.

When we first came here, and for the first few years, the happenings might well have defied belief. However, I have long held the view that it is possible for the personality of a person, or indeed of a family, to take over and predominate, in such a manner that previous hauntings might well be subdued; or become non existent. The property is rarely haunted now, with the important exception of the mental projection by the cat, and one or two minor incidents.

Now returning to the time when we had just moved into the property. Initially there were journeys backwards and forwards, involved with the move, and at times we would sleep here overnight and return to Cambridge on the following morning. We felt very relaxed here, right from the first moment. In fact, when we viewed the property, my wife dropped off to sleep in the little study, whilst the girls and I were looking at the grounds, and admiring the flowers. Out of interest, I mention that I have just called my daughter Julie, and asked her if at any time she ever felt any apprehension, and she said "No not at all, I would not have stayed in the house by myself if I had done, would I?"

Chapter 14

SHOT IN MISTAKE FOR A RABBIT

We had not been in the Old Rectory more than about two months after our move was completed, when my wife said that she had seen a tall woman dressed in an old fashioned style, standing on the top landing, at the servant's end of the house; and that she looked quite sad. At the time my wife described her, and said that she thought that she might be Mrs. Turner, wife of the first incumbent. She was seen only momentarily, and then was no longer there. On the following morning after this, we received a letter from an old friend of ours, in Cambridge, Rosie Mead, and in this letter she told how my old friend Stan Howe, was very ill in hospital, and was not expected to live. Therefore we decided to go and see him, on the following day. We found him extremely ill, but he was very pleased to see us, and said he was so glad that we had come. Unfortunately, he died within a couple of days.

We cannot know whether there was any connection between the sight of Mrs. Turner with a sad expression, and our friend Stan, being so ill. However, within two or three days of the lady being seen on the stairs, we received a transcript from the previous owners. This document contains the recollections of the old gardener, who worked here for many years. This transcript carries some description of Mrs. Turner, which agrees with that of the tall woman that my wife described.

I would like to return to Stan Howe. He was a simple man, of few words. There are some people whose company one can enjoy without the need for a lot of conversation. Stan invited me to shoot on his land, whenever I liked, and I used to keep down the pigeons and rabbits that ravaged his green crops. There was a deep ditch, which ran down one side of his property. I would often get comfortable in this, and shoot pigeon coming into the copse alongside. Stan had a ·410″ shotgun, which he hardly ever used. It was my practice to drive down to the bottom of the road through his property, where I would usually see him working about his greenhouses, or on the land alongside. There was an alsatian in a small yard, with a kennel. The dog served to guard the property, but the strange thing about this animal, was that it would bark to warn of the approach of anyone, with the exception of myself, and therefore on this particular evening, as usual, the dog gave no warning.

I looked in the various greenhouses, to let Stan know that I had arrived, but unfortunately did not find him. The reason for this was that he was hidden by the foliage of the tomatoes, which grew right up to the roof of the greenhouses. I made my way down into the ditch with my gun, and had soon fired a shot. Some while went by, when all of a sudden there was a rush of air around me, and a loud 'zing'. I realised that I had been shot. What actually happened, was that on this particular evening, Stan had decided to walk along the ditch to see if he could shoot a rabbit. He went straight from his greenhouse to his shed, where he kept his gun, and then to the ditch and did not see my Land Rover. While in the ditch, I wore a mask, darkish clothes and old grey gloves, and of course was quite still. Stan came along the ditch, and in his own words, "I thought I spotted the tail of a rabbit (my glove), and I fired." Fortunately most of the pellets went into the bank, but I still have seven or eight in my body. One flattened on the back of the skull, being still there. One in the elbow, and the rest generally down the left side of my body, and leg. Fortunately, they do not cause any trouble.

On the night that this happened, I asked Stan to drive me to the hospital in my Land Rover, but he was in a far worse state of shock than I was. Although the arm was painful, I drove home, and a neighbour then took me to the hospital. Poor old Stan paced backwards and forwards outside my bungalow, until my daughter Anne, persuaded him to go inside.

Most things have a humorous side, and this was no exception. When attending hospital, with gunshot wounds; there is generally an enquiry, in case of foul play. The official explanation for my accident was entered in the records as 'Shot in mistake for a rabbit.' There was no doubt that Stan was very shaken by this accident, and later he told me that his wife had said, "What did you want to go and shoot your best friend for?" We wondered if the shock of this very genuine accident, might possibly have been the cause of Stan's death. I realise that it worried him more than it worried me, as once the pain had gone, I felt no further concern.

Stan was a good man, working hard for his living, and charging only a very reasonable price for his eggs and vegetables. He was one of those Christians that rarely went to church. He laughed one day when he told me that the vicar had made his way to the fence and climbed over. He said "I thought I'd better come and see you, because I'm sure you'll never come and see me!" Sometimes I would take a bottle of cider to enjoy after the shoot. We would sit in the Land Rover together, talk a bit, and put the world to rights.

Chapter 15

CRINOLINE LADIES, CLOCKS THAT LOOK AFTER THEMSELVES, AND A BLACK CAT

The months rolled by, we were getting into a steady routine, and certain unusual things happened, although nothing alarming, or bothering. We have a good size dining room, which looks out onto a lawn; and each of its windows has a pair of hinged wooden shutters, which are used to cover the windows at night. These are secured with a steel arm and catch. Naturally, closing the shutters would always be a job for last thing at night. However, we soon discovered that it was not uncommon to find one of the shutters fully open, in the morning.

The Rectory, with the author and his wife on the lawn.

The shutters as they would often appear in the morning.

It is possible to overlook closing one, on one or perhaps two occasions, but after this we would be extra careful in making sure both were closed. However, we continued to find one shutter open, on at least six more occasions, and knew that there had to be another explanation.

* * *

During the summer, the younger girls used to ride their bikes to the village, where they would play badminton or table tennis. One summer's evening on returning up the side road, they both happened to look across to the lawn, where they saw two ladies in old fashioned crinoline dresses. They appeared to be in conversation. As soon as the girls came in, they told us about them. The 'Crinoline Ladies' could easily have been mental projections from two ladies who had enjoyed happy times at the Old Rectory (in years gone by), where they had probably played tennis or croquet.

H. Copnall

The 'Crinoline Ladies', by the Horse Chestnut tree.

On several occasions my wife has seen an old gentleman in our side wood; he was attired in the old style dress coat, with a flat hat (like the clergy wore), and gaiters. She has also seen a lady walking outside the kitchen windows. No doubt someone retracing steps taken many times before.

Soon after we came to the property, my younger daughter used to see an old lady lean over her, as if to make sure that she was all right, before going to sleep. On one occasion, she was working on the lawn, and heard voices close by, just as if people were working in the garden near to her.

The grandfather clock; one of four clocks and a watch which moved forward one hour without human aid.

We now come to a quite astounding happening. The room in which I am dictating was the old study; this we often use in the evenings. About two years after we came here, 1974, the girls were in bed, and we were watching the television, when the newsreader said "Don't forget to put your clocks forward one hour, tonight." At that time the little wall clock in this room said half past ten, so I stood up and moved the hands to half past eleven. We switched off the television and left this room in order to prepare for bed. As we went into the hall, I turned to the grandfather clock with the idea of putting it forward one hour, only to find that it already showed eleven thirty. Quite amazed, I called up the stairs to the girls to ask if they had interfered with it. They said that they had not. Just past the hall there is a drawing room, and this has a chiming clock on the mantelpiece. This clock still showed half past ten, but in fact, every other clock in the house, and including a watch which was in the scullery, had all been advanced by one hour; a total of four clocks and one watch. These had all been advanced one hour, without any assistance from us. At first my wife and I did not believe the evidence of our eyes; had we imagined it? But we realised that this was not the case.

The chair by the fireplace. Its usual place.

On going to bed that evening I was making my way to the toilet, when I heard a quavering voice call "Henry-y" and going into the bedroom where my wife was about to undress, I was shown that the small chair (that normally stands by the fireplace), had been moved, and put by the window. This chair is only used by my wife to put her clothes on when undressing, and is never moved other than by a person cleaning. There had been no-one in the bedroom, other than ourselves since the previous night, and therefore, there was no normal explanation for the chair having been moved.

The chair by the window, where it was moved to by night time.

The moving of the chair seemed to be someone saying – Well, if you don't believe the clocks, how about the chair!

One might ask, was there some sort of message here? I think undoubtedly someone was trying to make their presence felt, without alarming us unduly. I have read about four books on ghosts and hauntings, and can remember seeing a photograph of a clock in one, and there was mention of occurrences with clocks, in others. However, it does not seem an uncommon phenomenon.

The grand**mother** clock which did not need winding.

If the reader will have a look at the photographs of the grandmother clock, they will see one of the clocks that moved on an hour without human assistance. Another convenient peculiarity of THIS CLOCK was that although it is only an eight day clock; during a period of about a year, most times that we tried to wind it, we would find that it was fully wound, or nearly so. There was no question about this. It was not a case of another member of the family winding the clock.

* * *

There was a repeated happening, which occurred soon after we came here, and mainly before my eldest daughter went off to be a nurse. A black cat frequently came through the back door, through the passage and into the kitchen. On one occasion this cat (in spirit), came through, and our own cat saw it, hissed and bristled up. This witnessed by my wife and eldest daughter. The black cat has been seen to come through these rooms by all members of my family, except myself.

Soon after coming here we were tidying up in the wood alongside the road, when we came across a black cat that had no doubt been killed by a car. On making enquiries, we learned that the previous owners of this house had owned a black cat, which was rather wild; living mostly outside, and which they were unable to catch before moving away.

* * *

Although I am aware of various unusual incidents, involving other people, I have generally restricted this book to accounts of first hand experiences of myself and or the family; however, these are often corroborated by other persons. With regard to the various occurrences in and around The Old Rectory, one might say, "Yes but these were only seen by yourself, or your family," although we know these to be absolutely true. I will recall two happenings that were described to my wife and I, by Rosie Mead, who was mentioned in a previous chapter.

It was nearing Christmas time on the second year after moving in, and we thought that it would be nice if our old friends Rosie and Alex could come down and stay with us for the festivities.

One evening we all relaxed in the study, with a drink, and talked over old times, and eventually made our way to bed. Some while after retiring Rosie became aware of the sounds of happy voices, and music, which went on for some time, and she felt that the children must still be up enjoying themselves, but thought it strange because we had not gone to bed very early. In fact at this time we were all in bed, and probably asleep. Although this was Christmas Eve, Rosie did not drink any form of alcohol, as it does not agree with her.

The next incident occurred at about half past seven on the following morning. In order to appreciate this, I will describe the location of the two rooms mentioned. At this end of the house there is a passage which stops at a door leading into what was probably a servants sitting room. Immediately on the left as the passage ends, there is another door leading to the bedroom which Rosie and Alex were occupying. From Rosie's bed she could see through the door into the passage. On this morning, it was only faintly light, but the curtains were open. While still in bed she saw a man in a grey suit walk from along the passage, hesitate, look straight at her, and then go into the end room. Rosie did not see the features clearly, and so took this person to be myself.

Remembering this incident, and with the book coming to a close, I phoned Rosie to see if she could describe it once again for me, and was not surprised that she could remember the experience, in every detail, and reminded me that when she had first come downstairs on this Christmas morning, I had said to her, "Aren't you going to say good morning?" To this she had replied "I have already seen you once." In fact I had not been to that end of the house at all on that morning, and she had presumed that the man in the grey suit was myself, rather than actually recognising me.

* * *

Sightings of people and creatures in the form of apparitions are well recorded, and people or creatures in association with **inanimate** objects are not unheard of. When we lived in Enfield, perhaps about 1963, there was correspondence in the pages of the local paper (over a period of several weeks), concerning sightings (by independent witnesses), of a large coach and horses, complete with its lights, and the jingle of harness. This travelled over the route of an ancient highway, in the vicinity of the Enfield Rolling Mills. The letters were most interesting, and in fact one was written by the owner of a house which had been built across this highway; and every so often the coach and horses would pass through the wall of one particular room and out of the other side of the house. I mention this because these were well substantiated sightings and included an **inanimate** object, being the coach. It is because **inanimate** objects have been seen (as apparitions) in The Old Rectory, and by two different people, that these incidents are worthy of mention.

Over the first three or four years that we were here, I can remember my daughter Julie saying that on several occasions she had seen a walking stick in the downstairs toilet, at the end of the house; although none of us use a walking stick. Having experienced a number of such incidents throughout life, one does not take too much notice of them, and eventually the stick was no longer seen. Recently I mentioned to my eldest daughter Anne, the incident which involved Rosie Mead (described above), and she well remembered this. I happened to say that this experience in The Old Rectory, concerned someone outside of the family, and then she told me that her husband Steve, had also witnessed the 'Unusual' in our home. My son in law explained that it would be about three years ago, that he had seen a walking stick in the toilet, at evening time, and on going back later the stick was no longer there. The interesting thing about the stick, in both cases, is that it was not something which suddenly appeared and then vanished, as is usual with most apparitions. In fact, the stick remained there until the particular person involved, had left the room.

I was most impressed by the detailed description that Steve gave. He said that the stick was made out of one piece, and was very knobbly and worn; the general shape was that of a shepherd's crook, but without the hook section coming so far down, or being so pronounced, and the handle flared out into the shape of a 'T'. This description is very similar to that of a stick belonging to an old gentlemen that we knew, and his stick was knobbly, but without the 'T' shape to the handle, and being made from the stem of a Brussels sprout; which was often done, years ago.

Bearing in mind the description, and remembering that my daughter had seen a walking stick on several occasions; I thought this would be a wonderful opportunity to check if the stick that each one saw, was of the same description, and had appeared in the same position. Her stick had been seen on the left, by the door frame as one leaves the room, and it was straight and thin, more like a cane, and she said it could have been taken for a short length of billiards cue. Over a period of about four years she had seen it on several occasions, always in the same place and taking the same form, and remaining there when she walked out of the door. The difference with the sighting of the heavier stick, was that it appeared on the left of the small wash bowl, and leaning against the wall.

Here then are two accounts of similar **inanimate** objects appearing in the form of apparitions, (something seen, but having no material substance). How such objects **can** appear must be open to conjecture. Perhaps these were the walking sticks of a lady and gentleman, who resided here in the past, and somehow the image of the sticks is projected from this association.

The above incidents serve to show that persons outside of the family have experienced 'The Unusual', at The Old Rectory!

* * *

A lady who knows the house, and has worked here for many years, has mentioned some of the hauntings, and beliefs. She told us that when she worked here as a young woman, a local person had expressed surprise that she was happy to work alone in the property, when the owners were away. She said such things had never bothered her, and agreed that the Old Rectory has a very pleasant atmosphere.

The second rector lived here in the Rectory, with his unmarried sister. The story goes, that on one occasion he came back unexpectedly from the church (at the top of the road), to find a member of his staff, and his sister, in a compromising situation. Because of this, the rector is supposed to have set about the servant and sent him packing, chasing him down the driveway. Whether or not this is true we cannot know; but the driveway has been said to be haunted, at least, in the past. Certainly my wife has seen a woman (who could well be this lady), walking outside of the kitchen windows, at the top of this same driveway.

We learned too, that there was supposed to be a fear of passing by the bottom gates to the road, at midnight. We do not know the truth of these matters for ourselves. However, when we first came here, on several occasions, we would hear a passer by start to whistle or sing, as they reached our driveway. It seemed to fit in with the story; as if they were giving themselves some sort of bolster to their confidence, whilst going by this spot. Once past the gateway, the singing or whistling would stop. The house was empty for some while before we moved in; this may not have helped matters.

Perhaps twenty yards up from the front gate, there is an iron gate opening into a meadow, on the left. Now, this meadow runs alongside the drive which was reckoned to be haunted. On one occasion during those early years, I was standing with the horses, Ben and Jane, at a point just up from the meadow gate, and close by this driveway; when for no explainable reason, they bolted up the field. This was a bolt from a standstill, an immediate and spontaneous action by both of them together. By now, we had been with horses for over ten years, and I had never seen anything like this happen before. There was nothing to explain this sudden action. However, exactly the same thing occurred again some months later, from the same spot. The same spontaneous bolt by both horses. Whether there is any connection with the claims for a haunted driveway we cannot know.

All of the incidents mentioned in this chapter, took place within about the first three years of us being here in Suffolk.

* * *

There can be little doubt that the extra senses of animals are more highly developed than those of human beings, probably because of the likely inability to think. The family well remember an incident in Cambridge. At that time, we were grazing the two horses (Ben and Jane), on a large field just on the other side of the road past our property. The day was pleasant – bright and sunny although it was early winter time. At 3 o'clock in the afternoon we were working outside, and noticed that the horses were making their way to the gate. Once there they just stood. We went to see them, rather puzzled, as they would normally not come to the gateway until late evening, to be brought into the stables for the night.

Leaving them, we carried on with our work, but noticed that the horses made no move to go. By 4 o'clock the sun was suddenly blotted out by menacing grey clouds and we experienced a furious snow storm, with high winds which seemed to have sprung from nowhere.

Undoubtedly the horses knew what was coming, when all visible signs indicated a pleasant settled day. We hurriedly got them into the stables, and retreated from the storm.

The stretch of road where 'The Little Old Lady' was seen between 1974-1980.

Chapter 16

THE LITTLE OLD LADY

When I lived in Cambridge, I occasionally went pigeon shooting, locally; and in the Northampton area, and after coming to Suffolk missed my day out with the gun, and eventually arranged a day's shooting in Northampton. I had enjoyed a good day, and was fairly tired after a long drive, and returning home through the village of Brockdish. On the right hand side, there was at that time a small tumble down barn, or cottage. I had often thought that it was time that it was demolished, as it was close to the verge and might fall out onto the road and cause an accident. This was situated at a place where the opposite bank is quite high. There is really nothing along the road at this point, until the road bends, where there is a concealed driveway running back to the left.

Driving past this ancient building, I saw a little old lady, very frail and bent, facing ahead along the road, supporting herself on her stick and with her head turned, listening for the traffic. In her right hand she was holding a carrier bag, and she appeared to be dressed in an old raincoat. I noticed how frail she seemed to be. I had not passed her by more than maybe twenty yards, when I said aloud to myself "Henry, that person was not alive". On looking back there was no-one there. The reason why I came to this conclusion was because of the height of the bank at this point in the road, and that she seemed to be coming from nowhere, and would be crossing to nowhere that one might expect, since there were no houses or shops nearby. The height of the far bank and the continuous hedge made it impossible for her to cross into the opposite field.

I thought no more about the incident, other than to tell my wife, and more or less forgot it, until some while later when returning home on the same road, about the same time, and saw exactly the same thing once again, absolutely in the same position, quite still, with the same clothing and the same stance.

Now, some while after this, I happened to have an old friend of mine down here to stay overnight (Ron May of Chingford), as we were going out together on the following day. After his arrival, we had barely got into the drawing room, by a nice log fire and were talking, when I started to mention the little old lady; Ron interrupted me part way through my description of the old lady, and completed it himself, and said that he had seen her as he came through Brockdish. He described her as dressed in exactly the same way and standing in the identical position.

Another acquaintance was travelling in the opposite direction one evening with his son, and had a similar experience at the same spot. His son was driving when suddenly he thought he had knocked the old lady down. On stopping – of course – there was no-one there. The old lady was of the same general description and stance, although in the brief instant before the car appeared to strike her, he thought she was dressed in an old shawl, or even had a sack around her, but was definitely in the same position along the road.

It is likely that someone of this description had a very strong connection with this particular location.

Chapter 17

STRANGE HAPPENINGS IN NORWAY

There were three strange occurrences, when on holiday with my wife, in Norway. I can offer no explanation for them, other than to suggest that in a previous life, I may have had some connection with this country. I merely describe them for their interest value. May 1977.

We went from Bergen by boat, through the Hardanger Fjord, to Balestrand where we stayed at a hotel for some days, before travelling further up the fjord. From the second hotel we enjoyed several coach trips, one of which took us to see an old Norse Stave church. These churches are built around one or more staves, being complete tree trunks, going right from the ground, to the top of the tower. I had looked at the inside of the church, and then wandered outside, to a point perhaps twenty five yards beyond the altar-end of the church. From where I stood with my back to the church, the ground fell away steeply to a town in the valley below. It was a nice bright day and I was looking down admiring the view. Suddenly, there was an irritation at the back of my neck, just above the shirt collar, where it felt as if some pieces of stiff grass stem were being twisted to cause annoyance. Purposely, I did not turn round as I thought that my wife was fooling about. The apparent twisting continued; so I turned, to find no-one there.

Later in the same day we visited an area where extremely old farm buildings, and barns were preserved, in a sort of open air museum. These were very interesting, being of such old fashioned design that the roofs were comprised of turf. Once we had looked around outside, we went into a long building, containing a collection of very old style farm implements and farmhouse equipment. My wife had wandered off a little to my left and stood looking at the display, when without warning, I received an almighty push in the middle of my back, forcing me forward. Turning round, there was no-one to be seen.

Some might try to explain these two incidents as being imagination. However the last one to occur on that eventful day is not so easy to try to explain. Back in the hotel we cleaned up and then went into the dining room for dinner. There were four people at our table, my wife being opposite me. The food was always excellent at this hotel, and so I was thoroughly enjoying the meal, when suddenly my right foot was doused with water. Quite unquestionably, my sock and upper foot were very wet, and yet there was no apparent explanation. As I write this, I am wondering how many other persons have similar experiences, and perhaps are too afraid of ridicule to tell about them.

Chapter 18

THE GLASS OF PORT THAT MOVED

Let us pass right through the years, to about the end of 1981. By this time I had become involved with the parish council, and on one occasion had to go to see the clerk about a matter concerning rights of way. I took some paperwork along so that we could look at this together. It was the weekend, and he had company. Because of this he asked me into the kitchen, where we sat on chairs facing each other, both being alongside a formica topped table; one side of which was against the wall. At the back of the table were some bottles of wine and spirits which had been used for his guests. He asked if I would like a drink, and we both had port. After taking the usual sip or two, we rested our glasses down on the table. We had said a few words, and were sitting thinking about the matter in hand, when his glass of port moved steadily towards the wall, a matter of four to five inches. Its movement was not jerky, and was just as if someone was pushing it.

His head came forward as he exclaimed "Have I had too much to drink?" I replied "No I think **they** are trying to tell us something!", and said "Have you got a spirit level to check if the table is level?" He went outside and returned with a near new builder's level. On checking, the table was found to be **exactly** level in both directions. This did not surprise me in the least.

Of course, this sort of happening can have an explanation, other than that of having been brought about by some contact from the spirit world, or by extra sensory powers. I can see that if there was a perfect seal between the base of the glass and the formica of the table top, that water, or port, could be trapped between the base and the table top, in which case the glass could be held just slightly off of the table, when maybe it could move. In fact, this could not have been the case, because the table top was quite dry.

The other possibility then, is that with a perfect fit of glass to table top, that maybe air was trapped between the two; but even if this were so, I would not expect the glass to travel in an exact straight line, at a perfectly controlled speed. Obviously this is one of those happenings for which we may never know the answer, but never the less quite impressive to those witnessing it.

Chapter 19

THOSE WE ARE CLOSEST TO

I have read of a belief that when we die and move into an uplifted form of being, that we will be close to those that we were closest to on earth. I feel that this is highly likely. There are some people with whom one achieves a closeness, and may not necessarily realise it at the time. Many persons (like myself) may feel a closeness to someone who is no longer alive, in this world, and yet who may seem very much alive to us. Normally, I cannot easily visualise people by calling their exact features to mind. However, since becoming involved with the writing of this book, I seem to have built up a connection with those people mentioned in it, and to a much greater degree than I have experienced before.

My young brother (24 when he was killed in 1964), seems ever present and I see him in a way perhaps difficult to describe, inasmuch as I am not looking with my eyes, and yet clearly see him, presumably within my mind, and always (like the others), on the left.

Another person who is often with me, and occupies the same position, is 'Old Cressee'. I always seem to have a vivid mental picture of her, and am not surprised, because we must have been very close, although she was getting to be an old lady when I was quite a young lad. My sister and I were really favourites of the three Cressee Sisters. Emily was much like her sister Edith. I can remember her taking us for a walk through Broad Walk, many years ago, before it was made up to join with the Bourne. She became ill and died when we were quite young. Gertie Cressee, another sister was also good to us children, but we saw little of her, because she was mostly away, being a cook housekeeper in a titled lady's house.

Old Cressee, to us, actually Edith Cressee lived in Compton Terrace, Winchmore Hill, the house where my father lodged before he met my mother.

I got to know Cressee very well during the time that I did my morning paper round in her area, although as kids we saw quite a lot of her. On a Friday she would often come with my mother to meet us from school. We would go to the Triangle at Palmers Green, where

'Old Cressee.' Taken at the author's wedding in 1949.

we would be treated to tea or lemonade, and chocolate eclairs in Lyons. We often bought a great favourite of mine – currant doughnuts, which have long disappeared completely from the shops, no doubt because they do not suit modern production methods.

When I started my morning paper round, I would go back to Cressee's when I'd finished and she would have tea ready, and something to eat. It is funny looking back, because at that time, one of my favourites was mouldy cheese, and Old Cressee would save such delicacies for me. I used to do a few small jobs for her, one of which was the setting of a couple of mouse traps under the kitchen range. This was an old house and had its quota of mice.

To be able to pop into Cressee's and warm up before pedalling home was ideal. In the winter, one got pretty cold and hands were numb. I remember one morning setting her mouse traps, when my hands were still numb, and letting one go on my fingers! Bearing in mind my liking for mouldy cheese, I wonder now, how we managed to find any for the mouse traps. As time went by I got to know Cressee even better, because my mother became ill and needed hospital attention for two prolonged periods of several months each, during which time I used to sleep at Cressee's house. My younger brother was looked after by some good friends of the family during these times. He was not very old, and when he came back from these good people at Luton (the Fensums), he sounded like a little old man, having picked up the local dialect.

Although quite old, Cressee never failed to get up early and go along to Chalkley's the bakers at the corner of the road, to get hot rolls for our breakfast, before I went out on my paper round. It was rather nice at that time, because one could walk round the back alleyway from Cressee's and along to the stables, where the horses were kept that were used to deliver the bread during the day.

I can remember one winter time, when I was quite young, seeing a toboggan on the top of a shed, in a garden a few doors along from Cressee's, and thinking how nice it would be to have one. I must have passed some remark, because the next time that I went to see her, she had got it for me, as it was no longer used. It was said of her that she would get the top brick off the chimney for us, if she was able.

In the evenings when I stayed with Cressee I would do odd jobs for her, also to amuse myself. On one occasion I investigated the sewing machine which had not worked for some time, and discovered that Cressee had found it to be getting a bit stiff, and had oiled it with linseed oil. The machine was quite solid where the linseed oil had hardened, and it was necessary to wash it in petrol, before she did any more sewing. Sometimes I would take the cover off of her battery wireless set, and give it a good dust out, and cleaning the various contacts, plugs etc. One of her greatest pleasures was to listen to the Palm Court Orchestra on a Sunday evening, with me. It was surprising how trouble free that old battery set of hers was. Of course she only had her old age pension, and one of her difficulties was to find enough money to buy the high tension, and the grid bias batteries, and to keep the accumulator charged. Some of my most pleasing memories are of lending Cressee ten shillings on a couple of occasions, and also of receiving a similar loan in return, when I was a bit short myself. It must surely be a privilege, when a youngster can help out a grown up.

Over the fireplace in her home, was the lovely old Verse – "The kiss of the sun for pardon. The song of the birds for mirth. One is nearer to God in a garden. Than anywhere else on earth." 'Old Cressee' was one of those people who had achieved a spiritual existence on earth. She had no use for church, practising Christianity in her daily life. Of church, she said – "They will not get me there until I'm carried." Eventually of course, **they** did.

While writing this chapter, I have been pleased and surprised at the contact it has brought. When dictating with regard to Cressee, I was suddenly aware that I had a mental picture not only of her, but of her sister Gertie, to her right; complete with a hat I recognised, and a short veil, also full details of her lined face. It was just as if she was saying – "Don't forget me." On the following morning I became aware of another person looking over Cressee's shoulder to her right, and immediately recognised her as Emily Cressee, although until this moment I could not even faintly remember what she looked like.

Bearing in mind that which I have written concerning the memory bank of the mind, I can see that given the right conditions, it would be possible for me to have seen the other sisters, by pictures coming from this source. However, I think not in this instance.

Chapter 20

HEALING

The reader will recall how I received help (spiritual healing) from Mr. Wesley in connection with my eye problems, also the help with regard to the scout, and again when our daughter was so ill. See also Chapter 27.

It was after a healing meeting with regard to my eyes, that on returning home I sat down in an armchair in our living room in Linden Gardens Enfield. I put my right hand on the back of my head, much as one does when relaxing. While I was being healed by Mr. Wesley or any one of his team, I found that as they passed their hands over my body, the part being treated became hot. On this particular evening as I sat in the chair, I started to pass my hand over my head, without any conscious thought, and I noticed that my head became quite warm. At the time I sat in the chair, my wife was facing me and standing ironing. She did not look at all well, and I knew that she had suffered from a non stop headache for the last three days. As I passed my hand over my head, this continued to become warm, and I wondered if possibly some of the healing power had rubbed off onto me, from the healers who I had been in contact with. At this time I had been not been told by a medium that I could heal, nor had I read anything about it. No-one taught me to **WILL** my hands to lift and yet not to allow them physically to do so. Indeed, I have never spoken to a healer about this, to know if this is what is practised. I have already suggested that when power is interrupted in its normal path, that it appears to take another direction. Whether or not this is so with the healing that I have tried, I cannot know, but it seems likely.

What I did that night, was to stand behind my wife, put my hands on her head, and then I **willed** my hands to lift, and yet did not allow them physically to do so. My eyes were shut, and suddenly I could feel an upward movement taking place, as if my hands were lifting and taking my wife with them. In fact, they had not moved. This sensation is very positive and unmistakable, and I have found that when it is achieved, there is often a definite result. After the lift I could sense that my wife was falling, so I opened my eyes and then supported her, as she had momentarily fainted. It was as if I had become one with her. The collapsing was as plain to the senses as if it was happening to myself. The headache had gone without the slightest trace.

When we were living in Cambridge, one of the girls had most persistent earache. Although it was treated, it was still causing quite a lot of pain and keeping the child awake, crying at night. Without any real thought about it, I laid down alongside her on the bed, and put my arm around her, putting my right hand over her ear. I then carried out the same procedure as already described, and almost immediately she started to breath extremely deeply **almost gasping**, and went into a very deep sleep. The earache had completely gone when she awoke on the following morning.

On one occasion (where I was working), there was a young man who had suffered from severe neckache, for about three days. I tried straightforward massage on him, digging my fingers into the neck, and this produced an immediate cure.

The unfortunate point about healing, is that this ability may be dormant in most people, but is only practised by comparatively few. For my part, I lack the confidence that I might be able to help, and therefore am unlikely to try, on those other than my immediate family or associates. I believe it is considered that healing is achieved, not by the healers themselves, but by the powers that are channelled through them, from good souls in spirit who wish to help us.

In the case of absent healing, I believe a person capable of healing may only need to sit down in quiet surroundings (even to the point of stopping the clock), and concentrating their thoughts onto a person or creature who needs help. My wife and I have tried this on occasions, sitting down together, and concentrating, to try and achieve some benefit for the sufferer. Even if no good is achieved by this, it is a sure thing that no harm is done.

For those successful attempts that I have made at healing (some of which I have described), there are plenty of times that I have tried, and could not achieve the sense of lift, and then no benefit to the sufferer. This is of course as applied to my poor attempts. However, the power to heal seems to be much more readily available, when one is not overworked or over tired. Much the same as we find when going about our daily work. We cannot burn the candle at both ends.

I did ask Mr. Wesley on one occasion about faces that one sometimes sees formulating in one's mind. Both my wife and I have experienced this, and it may not be uncommon. In fact, what happens is that one might be sitting quietly, maybe a little tired, when a face will form in the mind; someone quite different to anyone we know. As we study it, we find that it builds up into a clear and detailed picture, as if we were within a couple of feet of this person's face. Mr. Wesley said of these people, that healers believe they may be coming through for help, in some form or another.

Chapter 21

DIVINING

At the first meeting with the lady medium she asked if I knew that I could divine. I said that I was unaware of this, but subsequently I tried divining for water and to locate drain pipes. Although I do not have great confidence in my abilities, I appear to be able to do this.

Naturally I found divining interesting and so my wife borrowed a book from the library, in which an army officer wrote at length with regard to water divining, and also the use of the pendulum, as opposed to the divining rods. He also discussed spiritual healing, all being allied abilities. This officer had been employed by the Indian Government for a number of years to locate water, and could do this with great accuracy and prediction of the likely flow from any one source.

It is believed that many people can divine, and in fact many of these extra sensory abilities may lie dormant in most of us. When one picks up divining rods and tries to get reaction to a hidden drain or an underground stream of water, my experience has been, that initially the divining rods might be **too** keen to move, rather than to remain inert. This could well be brought about by an over active mind subconsciously making suggestions, as to where the drain or underground stream might be. I am no expert on this, and would advise those who are interested to obtain a book on the subject.

When one tries divining or finding a lost object with a ball pendulum, then I think this is one of the most confidence shaking methods that one could possibly use. Having said this, I am well aware that the pendulum can be extremely effective, and it is certainly not unheard of for a diviner (using a ball pendulum), to assist the sober body of the police, in finding a lost person. I must confess that the ball pendulum gave me no confidence, until one day when we lived at Cambridge, I was unable to find our big pair of scissors. These had gone missing for a week or so, and now we needed them.

Just in case the pendulum might work for me, I thought I would try it. Remembering the instructions – one uses a ball suspended on a piece of thin twine, about ten inches long; this length being fairly important. What one does then, is to hold the pendulum (in my case a miniature billiard ball), in front and suspended from one hand. The diviner concentrates on the ball (which is stationary), and then mentally moves it around to swing in a circle. Surprisingly, when you do this, the ball **does** start to move and swing in a circle. Whether or not the mental activity is transmitted to the muscles of the hand and arm and this causes the swing, I do not know. After the rotary motion is achieved, one thinks of the lost item (in my case the scissors), and probably the pendulum will change its circular motion into a definite swing backwards and forwards, indicating a direction.

I tried this experiment, and after achieving the circular motion concentrated on the scissors. The pendulum changed its circular motion, to one of a definite swing backwards and forwards, in a positive direction. With some derision, I noticed that the direction indicated, pointed through the wall of the room I was standing in; there was nothing on this side of the wall. Ever willing to try, I went into the next room and stood in line with the swing of the pendulum and noticed that this cut right through the end of our settee, and surprisingly, the scissors were under the cushion.

More recently a key was mislaid, and for several days I tried unsuccessfully to find it. Thinking that this key must be inside the house, I tried the ball pendulum. After the usual circular swing, the ball indicated a definite direction; in fact straight through the wall towards the room being decorated. Looking on chairs and ledges etc. in line with the swing, the key was not to be seen.

Clearing up on completion of the decorating, I discovered the key hidden in the folds of the dust sheet, which had been spread to protect the carpet. The swing of the pendulum had indicated the exact line where the key rested, although I had not looked carefully enough to find it.

Through the pages of this book, we have seen that it is sometimes possible to experience and receive help in ways which we may be unable to explain. However, this lack of explanation should not be allowed to become an obstacle in our daily lives. Running along behind the stables, we have a ditch which is generally quite dry; but this year, because of the constant and heavy snow falls the ditch became completely full of water once the thaw set in. The water did not run away for some weeks and although this did not particularly matter, I made a mental note to locate and clear the drain pipe once

H. Copnall

The course of the drain.

the level had gone down. Just a few days ago now (being early April), I remembered the drain and the need to clear it. I must say that this drain had not blocked before, and I had no idea what form it took or at which point it entered the end of the ditch.

The ditch I am describing, runs from the top of the field, down behind the stables, where it ends abruptly against a hedge that surrounds a lawn at the rear of our house. Just at the point where the ditch stops, there is a small gap in this hedge, giving access to the lawn. From information received when buying this property, I knew that earthenware drain pipes should carry on from the end of the ditch, passing under the lawn to the far side, and then connecting up to a ditch running outside the hedge on that side of the lawn. Behind the ditch are some fairly large trees, and over the years the leaves have fallen into it and rotted, the entrance to the drain becoming completely covered. I got down in to the ditch and started to poke about with a piece of steel rod, but could not locate the end of the drain. Not wanting to dig more than was necessary it occurred to me to use my divining rods to locate the position of the drain.

By now the reader will realise that my approach to these matters is that of an ordinary man, certainly not one who claims to be an expert. First of all, I tried the rods from the ditch, but with indecisive results. It then occurred to me that from this position the rods were only able to be influenced by the end of the drain, and therefore it seemed a much better procedure to go a few yards on to the lawn to see if I could plot the exact path of the drain, (by standing above it) and then project this path to a point where it entered the ditch. Once I tried this, at every sweep the rods dipped very positively at one point; then I took a short step forward and tried again. After the rods had dipped four or five times, I could plainly see they were indicating a definite line pointing to the left-hand side of the end of the ditch. Going back into the ditch with my steel rod, I pushed this into the mould and immediately produced a metallic sound. On investigating I found an old cast iron grating which covered the end of the drain, and which was well hidden between tree roots.

The mundane task of locating a hidden drain can take some time and effort in digging; but the divining rods had given me the necessary information in perhaps no more than one minute, when I was able to go straight to the drain where this entered the ditch. In the days when there was not a piped water supply, a diviner could always be found somewhere in the locality of a village, and he would locate water for the village pumps and for households, as a matter of course. These old skills tend to be lost, but the ability to divine and heal is often present in most of us; and when the need arises, perhaps we could all benefit by trying them.

As the illustration for this chapter was being finalised, I re-checked the path of the drain in order to indicate its position. Some days later a son-in-law was with us, and I asked if he would like to try divining. Although he did not know how this was done, he was keen to try so we went to the area of the drain. Initially (as is not uncommon), there was no reaction, but after several passes I could see that he was beginning to detect the drain. Instructing him to move the rods to either side when he felt some activity, he was able to determine the point at which the reaction was greatest, and also to feel this diminish as he moved the rods away; thus pin-pointing the path of the drain. Within half an hour of actual dowsing, I asked him to plot the course of the drain. As he worked, it was plain to see that the reaction he achieved was indicating the same slighly curved course that I had originally plotted. I further checked him where the drain pipes meet at a sharp angle, and his findings were again the same as mine, that this is the junction of three pipes with one branch (to the left of the illustration), going approximately 20 yards to connect up with a hand pump against the wall of the house.

For those who would like to try the fascination of dowsing, there are usually good books in the public library, and there is also a British Society of Dowsers whose address would be available from a reference book (such as Whitakers), again in the public library. From this society it is usually possible to buy dowsing rods, although where possible one can cut a hazel or willow rod from such trees. The two arms of the 'Y' should be as nearly even in thickness as possible and the overall size being 12″–15″. The thickness could be approximately ½″ at the junction, tapering down.

One should bear in mind that diviners, like mediums, almost certainly need to clear their minds, in order to be receptive. Because of this, good results are unlikely to be achieved under test conditions; which are of very little value in these matters. The diviners of years ago would find water (for the villagers), as part of their normal work. Indeed, if the diviner could not find water, then **this** would have caused comment. Before piped water, and mains electricity were available, there was a great deal more trust in such arts, and adverse influences would have been near non existent, making the task easier.

Chapter 22

HAUNTINGS, SPIRITUAL VISITATIONS ETC.

I feel it is likely that when we die, we cast off the physical body, but retain all the senses in a much enhanced form. I believe also that in the usual way a person passing into the next life, will probably retain few ties with this one, unless there is a particular reason why they should do so. It seems likely that if there is a particular connection built up with a place, through very happy associations, or indeed through very sad ones, or perhaps a happening such as a violent ending, that in these instances, a person who has passed on (into spirit), may return to this earth in projected form.

As for the periodic re-appearances, I believe these are purely associated with the memory bank of the mind, and for some reason, every so often will re-appear from this source. However, there are undoubtedly other forms of visitation (possibly that of Mrs. Turner on the top landing), which may be brought about by the person in spirit wishing to make contact, although again it generally seems to take the form of a (non aware) projection, much like that from a movie projector – either still, or moving. At these times it is **not usual** I think, for any message to be passed on, or for the facial expression to change, although the expression itself may convey something. No doubt if a medium was consulted, the reason for the contact might well be established.

There are many and various hauntings. I read of an old public house which was associated with smuggling; at times there are heavy footfalls, and the sound of shots as if from the pistols of the excise men. All these visitations, could be brought about from the memory bank of a person, in spirit who may project either by design, or subconsciously. The reader will recall that I heard the voice of my brother, whilst I was mowing. Because of the loud noise of the mower, I tend to think this was a message transmitted to the sound section of the brain, and not through the ears. In exactly the same way, sound could be transmitted to a group of people, much as mass hypnotism is achieved. However, I am not suggesting that sound cannot be transmitted from the spirit world, for the ears to receive in the usual way, as we do not know this for certain.

It may normally take fairly exceptional conditions to produce an **intentional** and direct projection of the mind, which is then received as some form of apparition or voice contact. Such projections may occur when a person is contacted by a parent at the point of death. Or when there is a great feeling of needing to make contact, as in the case of my young brother after his accident. There have been numerous accounts of such happenings.

I hope the reader will agree that apart from my first two experiences, the contact with the spirit world has not been at all frightening, but certainly very enlightening and educational. I am convinced that people who lead a decent life, will rarely be bothered by those in spirit, ever around us and waiting to help, if we will let them.

Sometimes we read of hauntings which do not run to the usual pattern – the visitation of a 'Bad spirit' or perhaps a 'Jovial one', playing pranks. Poltergeists have been recorded many times, and are believed to tap an energy source such as that of a young child, to help move objects etc. (This theory agrees with that expressed in Chapter 25. Power of the mind.)

Undoubtedly there are the occasional 'Bad spirits' in the same way as there are bad people; but these represent a very small proportion of the helpful ones all around us. A medium once explained, that one's own life style and beliefs can create their own protection from bad spiritual influences. This does not seem unreasonable as we are well aware that those who mix with bad company in this life, generally become tainted by it.

Good mediums seem to be a readily available means by which persons in the spirit world are able to communicate with us, as I think has been amply shown in this book. I cannot think it could be in the plan of things for contact to be any easier. Don't seek the services of good mediums lightly, and remember the value of the results are likely to be a measure of your own faith and trust.

To sum up, it seems likely then, that any particularly poignant or exciting memory or an association with a place or person, may result in an image being projected, by person or creature (alive or in spirit) and this image may be accompanied by sound or smell, or both.

One thing that has become evident through the pages of this book, is that the old fashioned view of ghosts or spectres, only appearing as whispy, white, glowing creations appearing in the hours of darkness, should be discarded. Often an apparition may appear exactly as a normal living being or creature, and will merit no comment unless the sighting is repeated, or we know that the person we have just seen is not with us in this life. Another suggestion is that we should not look on houses as being haunted, as if this phenomenon is restricted to such places – **the world is haunted**. Spirit people are all around us and they may make themselves known anywhere; it is only perhaps because people spend a lot of their time in houses that the association is greater here. Remember the occurrences in Norway, the crinoline ladies on the lawn, the little old lady, the old gent pottering happily in the side wood, and all the others mentioned.

Chapter 23

IS THERE MORE TO A PICTURE, AND THE WRITTEN WORD THAN WE REALISE

E.S.P. AND ITS POSSIBILITIES

For some years, I have realised that a book can give me greater pleasure than one might expect from its written words. Sometimes I will be reading a tale – for example, one about the countryside, and I find that there will be pictures appearing in my mind. Perhaps the chapter takes one down a country lane, and in addition to the written word, a cock pheasant hurries across the verge to disappear into the hedge. The insects hum, and the grasses whisper as the breeze moves them. There are other additions to the written word as the story progresses.

Now, this makes for more interesting reading, but where do these extra details come from that so enhance the reading?

Ever since this phenomenon became apparent, I have thought it likely that the memory bank of the mind supplies the extra material, by association with the subject matter. But, in view of my recent experiences whilst watching television, one wonders whether possibly the written word (in itself) can convey additional information. We know that a medium can take an object, and from this can often give a great deal of information, which cannot be gleaned from the object itself, by actual study. On checking, I have found that other people can experience extra pleasures when reading, in the same way as I have described.

A similar thing occurs at times, when watching television and which I had perhaps wrongly associated with the memory bank of the mind.

Over several years, I became increasingly aware that scents and smells could come to me when watching the television. The screen might show a person smoking, and immediately the acrid smell of the cigarette would be apparent. One evening I watched a film about the pyramids, and when the burial chambers were shown, I experienced a most unpleasant dank earthy sort of smell. These are but two examples of many, over a long period.

I would not expect to smell these odours with my nostrils, and the only logical explanation seemed to be that the picture had activated that section of the brain concerned with the sense of smell, and the memory bank of the mind.

Perhaps my theories in this instance were wrong, as I believe a lesson may have been given to me.

A LESSON?

One evening I watched a film on television. At one point, I looked away from the screen, and suddenly the room was filled with the glorious scent of Carnations – unbelievably fragrant. On looking back to the television I saw a bunch of flowers laying on a table, and realised that they were in fact Carnations.

Just in case the significance of the Carnations may not have been apparent to me, a further incident occurred about two nights later, when the same lesson was repeated. Again watching television, but this time a quiz game was shown, involving various personalities. As before, I looked away from the screen, and became aware of a heavy sweet scent, like some Orchids. On looking back to the screen, I saw a well known television star, wearing a deep blue flower in his buttonhole. Within a few days of this incident, it was Mother's Day and one of my daughters arrived with a pot plant for my wife. A deep blue Cineraria, with the same heavy scent (at evening time) that I had previously noticed. The flower seen on the T.V. appeared to have a continuous petal arrangement, and could have been more in the style of a Morning Glory, but difficult to be sure in the brief time we saw it.

These startling revelations show me that a television picture (and probably an ordinary picture), is capable of transmitting scent, or that it is possible to receive scent in some way, from it. Don't ask me how this can be achieved, as in my case it just happened.

Is it possible that sound can be transmitted from a picture to make this aspect of E.S.P. more complete?

In the text, I have referred to a blind person who could tell the colour of an object by touch. This ability seems to be similar to the reception of scent described in this chapter. One wonders what more exciting lessons there are to be learned?

Chapter 24

REINCARNATION

I am convinced of the likelihood of reincarnation, and this is no doubt strengthened by my engineering ability. Right from my early days at school, engineering always seemed to be right for me. There were a number of skills which I appeared to have, and which I had not been taught. All through my life, anything to do with engineering has always gone right, with little effort. Whereas although I liked gardening, when I had more time; it was rare for me to get good results very easily.

There are various religions, including Buddhism, in which it is believed that the soul of man will be reborn as that of another person. I firmly believe that this is possible, and also that knowledge and skills may be passed on from a previous life. I have often thought that there was somebody watching over my actions, with regards to engineering, and making life easier for me in this respect. When I came out of the army I took a temporary job as a salesman in a motor cycle spares company. In those days engineering was quite different to the present time. It was usual to buy ball bearings loose; in fact just as many as one required. The salesman would go to the bin and take a handful, and then count them out. It often surprised me immensely, to be asked for thirty six, or perhaps sixty, and to put a quantity in a box and then to find on counting them that I often had the exact number – not one more, or less. Later in life when involved with engineering design, it would almost always be possible to achieve a perfect result first time, without any modification.

Although I firmly believe in reincarnation and also in the possibility of skills being passed on, I feel it is part of the plan of life, that we do not know who we were in a previous life, under normal circumstances. For example, I have been told on more than one occasion, and by different mediums; that I had been an extremely powerful person in a previous life. Imagine how frustrating it would be to know who one was at that time, when maybe, in this life there are difficulties which seem insurmountable in one's present status. It very definitely would not do, would it?

Chapter 25

POWER OF THE MIND

Over the years, one hears or reads of strange happenings that are apparently brought about by power originating from the mind. One hears of a young man who can materialise objects in the air. Another person can deflect a compass needle, by power of the mind. I have read of darkest Africa, that it was not uncommon for a witch doctor to **'will'** a native to die, and invariably he did die. I remember reading in a book of big game hunting, that a witch doctor put a curse on a native girl, and for some hours she was continually taking stones out of her mouth. This was witnessed by the writer of that book, and several very sane people, and for my part I would not doubt it. In fact the continuous materialising of objects is known to those involved with psychic phenomena.

Through the pages of this book, I think it has been shown that there are far more functions of the mind than we are aware, or understand. I wonder what would happen if fifty, a hundred or perhaps ten thousand people with spiritually developed minds, concentrated together for the purpose of healing. Also, could the stone blocks of the pyramids be lifted by the concentrated power of many minds, like some form of super levitation. Or, maybe this force of minds could achieve the same result more easily by neutralising gravity, or nearly so. In a similar manner, the recent spate of metal bending might well be attributed to a partial neutralising of the attractive forces which hold molecules together – all very feasible explanations in a field of intelligence where science holds no sway. We are unlikely to fully understand these matters until we pass into the next existence!

In the early part of this book I have said that progress and research in spiritual matters, and E.S.P. is unlikely to be achieved by a scientific approach. I am sure too, that it is rarely possible to give psychic or extra sensory demonstrations to order. Conditions must be right, and opposing influences should be kept to a minimum.

I would like to give an example of the wrong approach to research of these matters. Recently I watched a programme, mainly concerned with research into metal bending. As an engineer, I am aware that the explanations put forward were completely wrong. The reason given for the spoons and objects becoming soft and bending or breaking, was that these items had been bent backwards and forwards prior to the show. This is supposed to make the metal soft, so that little force is needed to break them. **UTTER RUBBISH!**

Any engineeer who has experience of the bending or forming of metals, will know that continual bending backwards and forwards does **NOT** produce a softening. Just the reverse! Metal subjected to this form of stress progressively hardens (known to engineers as work hardening), and becomes stiff and brittle, and generally distorts considerably before breaking.

It was noticeable, on the T.V. programme that the metal bent gently, and evenly; in fact quite differently to metal bent backwards and forwards, and which action has produced stress. Therefore, the explanations put forward to explain the phenomenon were **COMPLETELY UNACCEPTABLE** because they are contrary to the known physical characteristics of metals.

The study of a broken spoon in an electron microscope was sensible enough, but the conclusions were not! The microscope showed longitudinal cracks and smaller ones crosswise from these, we are told – exactly the same as are present when a piece of metal has been bent backwards and forwards continuously. The stated conclusion was that the spoon must have been bent backwards and forwards, before the show. Obviously, **preconceived ideas once again block progress**! The research simply has not gone far enough. Why does the scientist not look **for some other reason** why the spoon, or whatever it be, shows this type of fatigue pattern. Is it so difficult to take the view that it may be possible to produce **exactly the same fatigue faults**, by an entirely different method? It is quite wrong to give an opinion, without considering the possibilities of another force being responsible for the state of the metal. **This is not even original thought! How can we learn if we will not consider the likely existence of forces outside of our knowledge and experience, at the present time.**

I feel sure that metal bending is an entirely genuine phenomenon, with the exception of the odd trickster; and I put forward the theory that it is achieved by the power of the mind breaking down the attraction of molecules. Maybe this sounds far fetched, **but is it**? If the attractive force that holds molecules together could be weakened, one would expect a slight flexing of the metal to create the same fatigue structure as a continuous flexing would create in metal under normal conditions. However there would be a lack of distortion, as in fact is the case. Another convincing point is that a weakening of molecular attraction would certainly bring about a softening of the metal, which continuous bending cannot produce.

The possibilities of the power of the mind are endless, but man needs to lead a good life before he can realise the true potential, in the full use of it.

There are recorded instances in which objects have been held motionless in space, by the power of the mind; thus defying gravity. The deflection of a compass needle by the same means almost certainly shows that the earth's magnetic field has been influenced. The weakening of molecular attraction as suggested (in the section on metal bending) would therefore seem very possible, and the lifting of heavy objects by the power of many minds, may well be within our ability to achieve.

Chapter 26

FAMILY CONNECTIONS AND SIGNATURES?

As the writing of the book drew to a close, I wondered how our family story would be received. Also were there any points that I had not covered properly? Several copies of the text were given to various people to read for their interest, and to assess their reactions. From this, I was pleased to learn that my family and I, are not alone in experiencing unusual happenings; and it became evident that these happenings, like our own, may be predominantly concerned with their own family connections.

We have a good friend of my daughters, living close by; probably a more conventional Christian than myself. It was to this lady that I went to find the exact source of the various quotations that I have used in this book. Whereas, I know a lot of quotations, I am sometimes unaware of their exact wording. Although I know all that is recorded in this book to be true, I felt apprehensive as to the reaction it might receive from the older generation, as they often seem reluctant to talk about such matters, and sometimes go completely quiet at the first mention of anything a little unusual. I was very pleasantly surprised to find that the text matter had been well received, and indeed I was sent a three page letter concerning happenings which the lady has known of, and connected with her own family. These are very interesting and some have similarities with our own; and serve to show that families (besides ours), do experience spiritual contact throughout their lives. (See letter – addendum to Chapter 26.)

I have said that many of these occurrences seem to be directly concerned with the family. This can be expected, since if we were close to persons before they died, then if they are able to help us, or want to make themselves known, what could be more likely? There are many accounts of persons making themselves known to a close relative, when at the point of death, and also there are many happenings which may bear the particular signature of a person in spirit. The early experiences at the Old Rectory were mostly associated with the past. However, when I consider the instance of the clocks going forward by themselves, and also the grandmother clock, that did not need winding for a long period; I wonder if these incidents have the signature of my own brother on them? He was a clever engineer (with a sense of humour), and always had such a ready ability to grasp any matter concerning engineering, not needing to try very hard to produce excellent results. Like myself, he would often make a special tool, with accuracy and finish where required, and wasting no time on that which did not matter; thus producing very good results in a minimum of time. I can remember making a special cutter on one occasion, called a woodruff cutter, for machining slots in metal to within fairly close limits of accuracy. My brother studied this tool, and enquired of me if it was to cut wood – rough? I have wondered while writing, if in fact he has found it relatively easy to make his presence known through mechanical objects, such as the clocks.

Earlier on, there was another strange occurrence with regard to the clocks, which in fact I had discarded and did not intend to include in this account, until the signature aspect occurred to me; I had been sitting in the study dictating, and got up to stretch my legs. Going out into the hall, the grandfather clock (which appears in the photograph), had stopped at 10.30 a.m. This clock does not normally stop unless the weight has reached the bottom of its travel. It had not, but since the clock has stopped on very rare occasions, I did not think anything of this. I checked the time in the study, and then started the clock, moving the hands to the correct time, which was then 11.30 a.m. On going down the passage towards the kitchen, on the right there is a cuckoo clock. Now, the strange thing was that this clock was still going and yet it was one hour slow, and indicated the same time – 10.30 a.m. at which the other one had stopped. This clock does not have any loose hands, and there was no explanation.

I had decided not to include this incident, until I realised that there might be more to it than I at first thought. It occurred to me that if I had not gone into the hall at exactly 11.30, then the significance would not have become evident. Another thought came to me – that the two times – 10.30 and 11.30 are exactly the same as those which featured in the previous happening with the clocks. (Chapter 15.) The only difference being that on one occasion it was a.m. and on the other it was p.m.

It seems likely, that all of these clock incidents may well bear the mechanical signature of my brother, and probably have no association with this property in the past. The clocks can have no previous connection as they were either purchased after we came here, or in the case of the cuckoo clock, this was originally my mother's.

Of hauntings, one will hear – "If there was anything there I would have seen it, I've been there often enough", and such remarks. However, many people will probably never see or experience anything, if they do not have the right mental outlook or approach, and even then would need to be in the right frame of mind, I feel. To go looking for experiences, or expecting them is unlikely to produce any results, and in any event it may take a lifetime to experience anything unusual.

* * *

Although the book was near completion, I felt sure that there would be occurrences in the future; hence the title – THE UNFINISHED STORY. In fact the happenings continued, and there were two minor ones within one week, described below, and two more very significant incidents – one at Easter time 1984, and concerning healing, and one in August 1984, taking place in South Africa, whilst on holiday. These are described in Chapters 27 and 28.

To return to the more minor occurrences:– My wife and I were in our yard; this is separated from the meadow by a brick wall and small lawn. Suddenly we heard the sound of a horse galloping up the field to the stable area, and finishing on the concrete. There has been an enormous amount of rain this year, but the pounding of hooves was what one would expect to hear under hard, dry conditions. On going to investigate, we found that our two horses were grazing peacefully right down the bottom of the field; there was no evidence whatsoever of a horse having galloped.

At 1.30 p.m. on Tuesday of this week, 31.5.1983 I was just about to leave the yard to keep a dentist's appointment. I knew my wife and daughter to be down the bottom of the meadow, with the two horses, (being lunchtime). As I was about to get into the car, I was suddenly aware of the ring of horse shoes moving backwards and forwards on the concrete in front of the stables. My immediate thoughts were that for some reason or other the horses had been brought up to the stables. On investigating, there were no horses or people anywhere in sight, at the top end of the field.

'Goldie.'

To some – such happenings might appear highly imaginative. However, I think the reader will agree that one's mind is unlikely to be on the supernatural at the point of dashing off to a dental appointment!

The thunder of hooves of a heavy horse, and the ring of shoes on the concrete can undoubtedly be attributed to our fine horse 'Goldie' – he was quite a character, very heavily built, powerful and having quite a lot of Hanovarian breeding in him. His favourite pastime when turned out in the mornings was to make his way along the concrete, to the other two stables and gobble up anything that the other horses had left. At that time, we had three horses. He was also an animal to come up the field at full gallop to greet us, stopping at the last moment as one stood on the concrete at the front of the stables.

Goldie unfortunately was found dead in the stable one morning, having suffered a strangulated gut, not uncommon in horses. We had him for eight years; he was a boisterous and very loveable animal, being very relaxed with us; in fact I can remember one of my daughters laying down in the stable with him.

Goldie was very much missed; and I feel sure he has returned here, at least on the two occasions mentioned, in a form which we are unable to understand, or explain fully. The thunder of hooves of a heavy horse coming up the field, and the sprightly ring of steel shoes on the concrete of the stables as he sought an extra mouthful, very definitely bears the signature of 'Goldie'.

Chapter 27

REPRIEVE FOR A THOROUGHBRED

It was in August 1982 that we purchased a new companion for our old mare Jane. 'Ricky' the new arrival had been bred and trained as a racehorse at Newmarket. His real name being Pete Murray, being bred from Pete Moss on the one side, and Murrayfield on the other. His name of Pete Murray (as registered), not being particularly liked, he had acquired the name of Alaric – Ricky for short. Somewhere along the way, he had sustained an injury to a foreleg causing it to thicken, and being no further use for racing, he had been sold as a riding horse. He must have passed through several hands, before we purchased him. Once he settled in, he soon became very friendly and manageable, and some time passed with him giving pleasure, and enjoying being ridden.

It was just before Easter of 1984 that he was being brushed in our bottom field, during the lunch break. He was tied to a three foot wide metal gate, which had hinges in the manner of substantial eyes, slotted over long steel hinge pins. All went well with his grooming, as indeed it always had done, until something caused the horse to rear right up, and take the gate with him. What was the cause of this, we will never know, but it is likely that it was a sting on his underparts. It might have been some sudden movement of a creature close by in the ditch alongside, and which we did not see. However, he galloped off down the field, with the gate between his legs, with the result that he received a very severe cut to his underside; this nearly fifteen inches long, and right through the skins. Although, this was alarming enough, he had also sustained an injury to the stifle, or hip joint, of his nearside rear leg. This injury being in the form of a deep cut, about two inches long, and passing right through the capsule, which surrounds the joint. At that time, we were not aware of the exact structure of the joint of an animal (or indeed of a human being), but soon learned that the joints are surrounded by a capsule or sealed cup, kept full of joint fluid, or oil, in the same way as oil is used to lubricate components in gear boxes etc.

A description of this all important occurrence may not be readily appreciated by all, but necessary for the completeness of this record. Being called to the stable area, where the horse had been brought, I was quite alarmed at the quantity of blood which covered the concrete, and which would have been several pints; this issued mainly from the wound to the rear underside of the animal. A large pad of rag was quickly placed there, and held tightly against the injury to help arrest the flow of blood. An urgent call was then made to the veterinary surgery, and our young vet was quickly on the scene. The horse was taken onto the field, where it was softer, and anaesthetised before a major suturing operation was carried out to repair the damage to the animal's underside.

At this stage, the vet had decided not to attempt to stitch the stifle injury, feeling that any stitches would almost certainly pull out. In fact, in veterinary circles today it seems to be generally reckoned that stitching at this point, is not a practical proposition, due to the extreme amount of movement and stretch that takes place here.

For several days. we watched an otherwise healthy horse – not in any great pain at all, walk about, squirting joint fluid from the wound at every step; exactly in the same way as is achieved with an oil can. The stitching to the underside, had been perfectly successful, right from the very beginning and gave no further trouble. Several days went by, and the fluid issuing from the joint had not become any less alarming. Remembering that we had an old veterinary book, published in 1837, the writer started to look through the section covering similar injuries. It was surprising to find that in olden times, when horses were much more important to the economy, in agriculture; that most broken bones in the legs of a horse were reckoned to be curable, and that injuries to the stifle were often successfully treated. It is not perhaps that there is no humanity left, but that these cures were very much dependent on lots of cheap labour, which we do not have today. Some of these cures were achieved by the use of grooms in attendance on the horse, night and day, often continually for as long as three weeks.

Our young vet being a very humane man, agreed with our suggestion for an attempt to be made to stitch the capsule, probably because he respected our care of animals. He readily agreed that the animal was in little pain, and showed every sign of being a perfectly happy healthy horse. It was soon arranged that two vets would attend on the following day, and make the attempt. Shortly after their arrival, the horse was put under anaesthetic and the stitching was commenced. All went well, with the two vets working quickly together, until the animal suddenly regained full consciousness at least six minutes before the anaesthetic was expected to release its control. The treatment was then finalised by using local sedation.

After this treatment, it was decided that we would stay in the stable with Ricky, right throughout the night; this in order to make sure that he had no chance to bite the wound. The night went fairly well, with the members of the family taking turns at being in the stable with the horse. The night was shortened by cups of coffee, and sandwiches, and the horse was fairly quiet; I was getting a couple of hours sleep, resting on two bales of straw, against the wall. The horse was somewhat dopey with the various drugs which he had been given, but awake enough to move across the stable, and put his head right down to my face, to investigate the strange sound of my snoring.

The following morning, we devised a means of preventing the horse biting the wound. This was achieved by taking the rope from the headcollar along the right hand side of the animal, and securing it to a girth strap. Thus, we could adjust the rope to prevent the horse's teeth reaching the stifle joint. This would be all important as the wound healed, and started to irritate.

We had discussed with our vet, the possibility of the suturing failing. Quite rightly, he had suggested that if this happened, the only course of action would be for the animal to be taken into a veterinary hospital, and put under very deep sedation. If this were done, then the surgeon would be able to probe much deeper into the wound, and make a far stronger job of the stitching. Eight days passed, with Ricky appearing to be quite comfortable and with no loss of joint fluid. Then, suddenly the wound opened, and joint fluid started to jet out, every bit as badly as before. Later that evening, the vet phoned to say that arrangements had been made for the animal to be taken in on the Monday – about a week hence. I should say at this point, that I had spoken by phone with one of the senior partners of the veterinary practice. He said that he was sorry to hear of the re-opening of the wound, and suggested that we might soon have to think about putting the animal down, on humane grounds. However, he agreed that the horse was in no noticeable pain at that moment. I replied that while the animal was not suffering, we should continue the treatment, but once he showed signs of distress, then we would want him put down immediately.

We now come to what to us seemed to be a near miracle, although we are well used to strange happenings. We – the family had talked at length about the possibility of Ricky going into the veterinary hospital; with very mixed feelings. Whereas we had confidence in that which the veterinary surgeons would set out to do, we did not have confidence in our animal's ability to remain quiet after the operation, and in strange surroundings, with different people. Although a fine animal, and extremely friendly, he is somewhat nervous with strangers.

I have often said, that it is very wrong that we only call upon 'Spiritual' help, when we are desperate. One feels rather guilty in only requesting this form of help, perhaps as a last hope, I suppose we are only mere mortals, and tend to rely on that which we can see, rather than to have faith. I said to my wife that we ought to seek healing help for Ricky, as we had received great benefit, on previous occasions. She agreed, and while she sat at the typewriter, I dictated a request for 'Absent healing', to the Spiritualist Headquarters of Great Britain. I explained the situation – an injury which is not normally considered to be curable, and yet which the vets were doing their utmost to cure. I underlined our uncertainty with regard to the result, if the animal was to go into a veterinary hospital. The reader will recall, that the wound had reopened, and the joint fluid had recommenced to squirt out as badly as before.

We have always found it to be a remarkable thing, with absent healing, that if it is going to work, it is usually an immediate thing, or not at all. It was only the second day after dictating the letter to the S.A.G.B., almost before it could have reached them, that my daughter Julie came into the kitchen just after lunch time. With an expression of disbelief in her eyes she said, "Dad, come and see Ricky, his leg seems to have healed up". On examination, I saw that the skin at the point of the wound, seemed to have healed over, and there did not appear to be a hole, at all. It had taken on the appearance of a plucked fowl, being red and pimply.

We must not overlook that the stitches had lasted for eight days, before the wound had reopened, and the centre of the wound had parted to form a sizeable hole. There are considerable difficulties in getting the flesh to knit together at this location; because of the extreme amount of movement, and stretch that occurs. An even greater difficulty is experienced because the leaking joint fluid creates a barrier between the flesh, which needs to grow together.

'Ricky' the reprieved thoroughbred.

From this point on, the wound remained closed, and no further leakage occurred. However, there was one very noticeable difference with the horse in that he now suddenly developed a great love of sleep, and would still be laying down in the morning when we went to feed him. In fact, for a period of about three weeks, he would just lift his head as we opened the stable door, and then lower it, and carry on sleeping. Please note:– The horse had only developed this love of sleep since the request for healing help. Even just after the injury, and up to this time, he had been his normal self, in this respect.

My daughter Julie, being extremely fond of this animal, was very disturbed by the change in his habits. On several occasions, she found him so deeply asleep in the field, that he appeared to be dead, or very close to it. There is no doubt in our minds, that this was all part of the spiritual healing process, and after this period, he reverted **suddenly** to his normal ways. When we bought Ricky, he had a very noticeable oval shaped swelling just below the left eye, something like a wart or cyst perhaps. We were told that he had always had this slight abnormality; so perhaps our spiritual friends decided to give him an overhaul while they were at it, because within a week of the letter asking for healing help, this swelling had completely disappeared, and there are no signs that anything was ever there.

Unfortunately, our young vet moved to a new area just shortly after this happy conclusion to Ricky's problems. His love of horses prompted his move to a practice where he could work more with them. While he had treated Ricky, it was very pleasing, even during the worst of the horse's problems, that when the man who gave the injections and caused discomfort, came up the path; that Ricky still whinnied to him. There is very definitely an affinity between animals, and some people.

Before our vet left for his new practice, he came to say goodbye, and without any prompting, he said, "There was something, very unusual about the healing of your horse's leg". He had told me previously that he liked coming to us, and found my accounts of healing, and the supernatural, fascinating. As he sat in his car, just before departing, I said, "I expect you will remember me as a very strange old boy?" His reply was – "I shall remember you as a very wise one". I had, at the risk of offending, written to tell him of our request for spiritual help for the horse. We felt that we should, because there might just come a time when he would remember this incident, and maybe find the need to request similar help. Perhaps if not for an animal, then for a loved one.

After several months of rest, then careful exercise; the horse regained his vigorous vitality, retaining no ill effects from the injury and is regularly ridden.

Chapter 28

THE TWICE VANISHING IMPALA

Although I have had little time for sport, during a busy life, there have been some very memorable visits to the wildly beautiful places of this country, and more recently to those of South Africa. My wife and I, have found this vast continent so very fascinating, although we have only managed to make two short visits. I have never felt that there is anything wrong with manly sports, provided that they are carried out for the right reasons. Indeed, sport and conservation generally run hand in hand.

It was in 1980, that our family encouraged us to go on safari in South Africa. Doreen my wife, shares my love of the wild places, and needed little encouragement. In September we flew to Johannesburg, then travelling extensively over the Transvaal, during a fourteen day stay. This trip left a lasting impression on us, and ideas of returning were never far from our minds, in the following years.

I have always felt deeply moved by the natural beauties around us, and invariably have described these in account, or by verse. Perhaps the joy that one can experience in the wild places, is beyond description, but being moved by the African landscape, and its wildlife, I made the attempt in my poem – 'My Africa'. This written after our trip, in 1980. To take pleasure in the wonders of creation which surround us, brings a peace of mind which can transcend all other considerations.

Four years were to pass before we returned to our 'Eden', South Africa. Before describing our experiences, a brief description of the policy of controlled hunting, and conservation, may be of interest.

Controlled hunting and conservation together, has proved a wise policy, and has proved a great asset. Most of all, it is of benefit to the wildlife which the governments set out to protect. It is essential to be practical, and to realise that conservation can only work if put on a sound business basis. Before this was so, the extensive herds of antelope and various other species, such as the big cats, elephants etc., were being decimated by overshooting, and by extensive poaching, and this often cruel in the extreme. Also at times, war had taken great toll of the wild game.

A typical example of what can be achieved by such a policy, can be illustrated by a study of the present herds, and increasing numbers of the Black Wildebeest, or White Tailed Gnu. Before the advent of the early settlers, these prehistoric looking antelope had occurred in enormous numbers on the plains of the South Western Transvaal. The ruthless slaughter of this species, for meat and hides – often used for bucket making, had almost exterminated them by 1885. Fortunately, before total extinction had occurred, conservation minded farmers, and authorities were able to introduce some of these antelope onto game farms, and nature reserves. These Black Wildebeest have increased their numbers very successfully, and now the surplus can be taken by hunters, who pay a very substantial fee for the privilege. This source of income is then used to maintain existing reserves, and to establish new ones. Without this system, in time; almost all the herds of each and every species would disappear. Today, big game hunting pays the greatest part towards conservation, and indeed, some of the large societies which exist for the hunter, also contribute substantial sums towards preservation. Wildlife is big business, attracting the trophy hunter, those who hunt with the camera and the tourist, visiting the large game reserves. All contribute to make preservation possible. Properly managed conservation, and controlled hunting, will not only continue to protect the White Tailed Gnu, but all other species which are competing with the human race for their habitat.

I am now going to take you into the bushveldt, in the Faan Mentjies Game Reserve. This fine reserve, at Klerksdoorp (in a drier part of the Transvaal), is owned by the town, and run for the Town Council by a very kindly man, Hendrik Kotze, and is a fine achievement. For a large part of the time, no hunting is carried out, and never on Sundays. On some Sundays the public can obtain a ticket at the entrance and drive right through this extensive area, although they must keep to the roads. There is a fine picnic area available to visitors, where they may light fires in safety, and make their own braai (barbeque). On this reserve one can experience the vast size of the African plains, and enjoy the sight of the White Tailed Gnu, the beautiful Red Hartebeest, with its peculiar rocking gait, the distance covering Gemsbok – always moving away, the stately Giraffe and the prehistoric Rhinoceros, to mention just a few. The smaller animals are also very evident – Ground Squirrels, the various Mongooses and not to forget the Lizards.

Ostriches are common enough on this reserve, and the practice is made, of taking the young chicks soon after they are hatched, so as to save them from predators such as Jackals. Rearing these in pens until they are large enough to look after themselves, is a very good idea. While we were there, a batch of half grown ostriches were released into the reserve.

Looking back through this book, and indeed through our lives, it is evident that not too long goes by without something unusual happening. There was something about this second trip to South Africa, which seemed to enhance our values of spiritual matters, and create a greater accord with nature. Our professional hunter Jaap Seegers, will always occupy a warm place in our memories. A man with a greater understanding of creation, than most men will ever achieve, and an affinity with the creatures of the wild places. It did not surprise me therefore, that we shared a quite remarkable experience together while we were on the Faan Mentjies Reserve.

One particular morning, we had decided to go after an Impala, being one of the most common, and graceful antelopes of Africa. We examined several small herds at a distance, and eventually selected one group of about twenty animals. Most of these were females, but there were three very noticeable adult males, which could not be mistaken for each other, or for the youngsters in the herd. One of these was a 'Unicorn' – a male with one horn broken off, then there was a good male with widely separated horns, which we referred to as 'Wide horn'. Another good adult male had narrow horns, which we referred to as 'Narrow horn'. Using the truck to get reasonably close, and then foot, we spent all of the morning, and part of the afternoon in attempting to get within shot. A decision had been made to take the 'Wide horn'. For some time, we could not get close to the herd, but later on in the afternoon, we did eventually come up with it, and this time we were well within range. We were in an area of acacia scrub, and the Impala were moving between cover, whilst going to the right. Suddenly 'Wide horn' stopped in a gap between the scrub, and he could have been no more than 85 yards away. I was perfectly relaxed, and had an excellent rest, and took careful aim, and fired. It is usual with such a shot, that the antelope may run a hundred yards or so before dropping stone dead. At the shot, the animal ran to the right, but he was never found. In all, we searched for over two and a half hours that evening, and carrying on the following morning. Our professional hunter was sure that a good shot had been made, and

Jaap pointing out hybrids of his beloved Aloes.

indeed, in searching the immediate area, he found a furrow in the ground where the bullet had carried on after it had presumably passed through the antelope. A sighting was taken from this point back to the position where the rifle was at the time of firing, and he declared that the bullet had passed through the position where the animal had stood. In his opinion, it had been a perfect shot. Up to this point, nothing was particularly unusual.

By now, our hunter Jaap, was becoming somewhat puzzled, and indeed more than I and my companion (Ron May), were at that time. However, our next move was to find the herd, to check that 'Wide horn' was with them. Eventually we came up with the group, and although all other members were present, 'Wide horn' was very definitely missing. This was unusual, because a group generally stay together.

On the following morning, we searched once again, thinking that perhaps we had missed the antelope in the bush; although this was not at all dense. Being unsuccessful we decided to locate the herd. Some hours were spent before we actually came up with it, but once we did, it was in plain view no more than a hundred and twenty-five yards off, and showing up clearly against the barren side of a hill. There was very little cover, and we were able to see the slope, right across our front. Initially, the herd was to our right, and moving to the left, as the animals took an occasional mouthful of the parched grass. Eventually, the group was fairly stationary for a while, to our left, and then started to move slowly to the right in single file, and passing behind a small acacia bush. The Impala were led by the females and followed by the youngsters, with the older males to the rear. As we watched, we could plainly see the animals pass behind the small bush, and reappear on the right hand side. As the last few animals were to pass behind the bush, we could see 'Unicorn', and then to our great surprise, he was followed by **'Wide horn'**, and then 'Narrow horn' at the rear. Our hunter almost jumped with excitement at seeing the missing Impala – **'Wide horn'**, and the eyes of the three men of our party must have been almost literally glued to it. Imagine our surprise to see **'Wide horn'** go behind the left of the bush, but never reappear on the other side of it. 'Unicorn' had come out from behind the bush, and so had the last one in the line – 'Narrow horn', but **'Wide horn'** had vanished; we did not see this Impala again. There just was no cover, and there were no folds in the ground into which this antelope could have gone. In a state of great

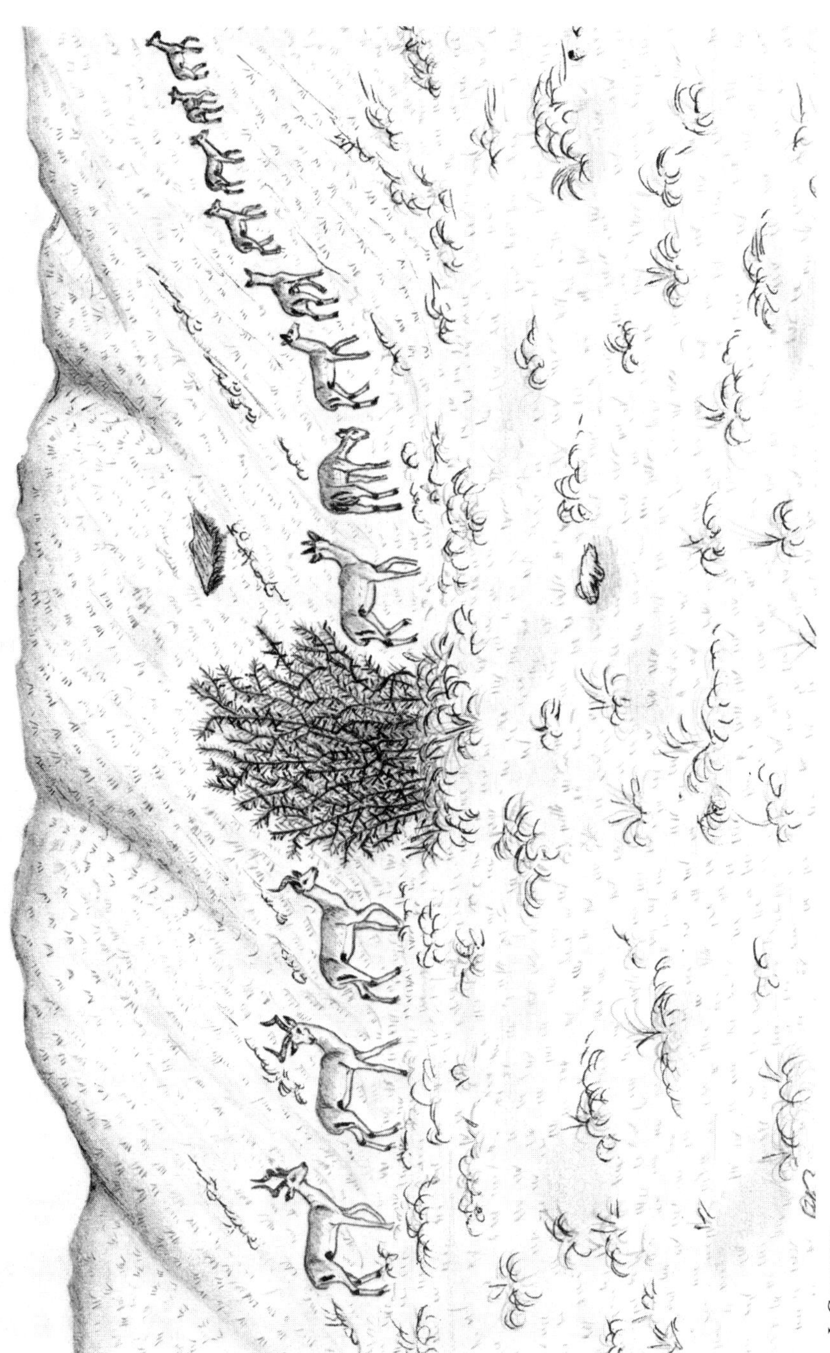

L. J. Copeman

'Wide Horn' about to go behind the bush.

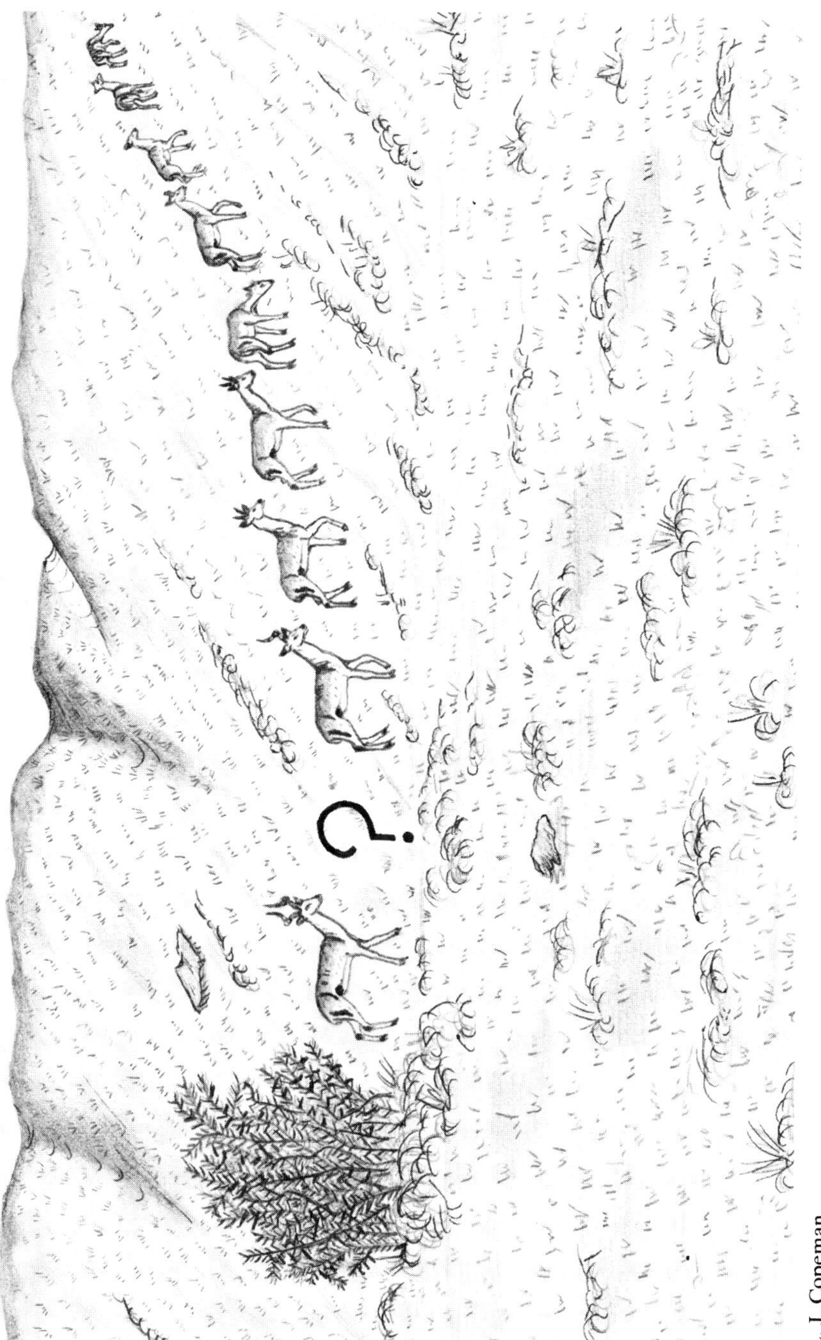

'Wide Horn' has vanished.

L. J. Copeman

My wife Doreen's birthday party, in camp. Mrs. Seegers and Ron May to the right.

puzzlement, Jaap climbed above the position, while we all spent some time in studying the immediate area, convincing ourselves that the animal had no available hiding place, on this slope. The bush itself was very small and only about the same length as the antelope themselves. **'Wide horn'** had just vanished.

I have expressed the opinion at some length, in this book, that persons and creatures will often appear, after death, and carry out the same actions which they commonly did when they were alive. I have also expressed the opinion that it is possible for a living creature to project its image. Coming back to our vanishing Impala, which had in fact vanished twice, we are faced with something of an involved mystery. If we accept that there can be no normal explanation for the second occurrence, where the Impala was plainly in sight, and then vanished; we must accept that we were looking at an antelope in 'Spirit form'. Regarding the first occurrence, the antelope could have **already been in spirit form**, whilst moving with the herd; or maybe we were just unable to find it in the bush. However, were we to accept this, then the same antelope – in spirit form, must have rejoined the herd later, in order to have been seen on the hillside.

Some months after returning to England, I received a letter from Jaap Seegers, our hunter, in which he says, "The mystery of the missing Impala is not solved yet" – in any event, what normal explanation is possible for such an event? He certainly has not seen 'Wide horn' again, although he has been onto the reserve on several occasions since. It may be that some might say that it could be easy to mistake one Impala for another, although this would not afford an explanation. One must remember that in this instance, we are always dealing with a missing beast, rather than a different one. I would say that it is quite remarkable how a professional hunter always knows a particular animal in a group, by noting small features which will be peculiar to this animal alone. 'Wide horn', had horns of an identical length, and which were exactly symmetrical; this being somewhat unusual.

Although the herd had been in full view for some while, as it moved leisurely on the hillside; 'Wide horn' was **not** present until that perfect moment, as the last of the antelope were to pass behind the bush. This made certain that the sudden appearance; and disappearance could not go unnoticed.

An experience such as this leaves a profound impression, which will likely remain throughout a lifetime. Jaap wrote, "I think that some of the happenings will stay with me for my old age, to chew on."

AN APPRECIATION OF THE UNIVERSE

POEMS

MY AFRICA

AWAKEN TO LIFE

MY AFRICA

Clear in my memory will always be
A far away place across the sea
Where the bush holds most that is dear to me
The birds and the beasts that wander free.

South Africa

A warm breeze blows across a land
Unspoiled by man's destroying hand
Where scents and sounds and spoor abound
And unseen eyes are all around.

Close by the dry Limpopo bed
An aged Wildebeest lies dead
No more to wander o'er the plains
Or follow the path of the annual rains.

Pontdrift

Creatures of death the Vultures feast
Upon this kill of a noble beast
Game now free to go its way
As Lions doze throughout the day.

Harsh it may seem, but nature's way
Makes strong survive for another day
Thus herd improves, and sickness rare
And weak and dying may not despair.

Ellisras

Delightful scent from orange trees
At dawn is carried on the breeze
Honey birds in blossoms play
As Orioles salute the day.

Monte Cristo

Tracking Waterbuck since dawn
Only glimpses through the thorn
Torpid Python by the track
As Waterbuck have doubled back.

Wylie's Poort

Eland browse with head held high
Thus hearing good, and watchful eye
Alarmed the big bull runs some while
There's safety in another mile.

Transvaal

Burchell's Zebra graze the plains
Blue Wildebeest and other game
Talking herds, with bark and grunt
A peaceful scene 'til Lions hunt.

Pontdrift

By river bed and Jackal's lair
The Eagle's call upon the air
Insects hum, the hours pass by
And Geese wing on the evening sky.

Potgietersrus

A Sable Antelope, quite still
Against a rock-face on a hill
Stately Kudu pick their way
As sun goes down at close of day.

Pontdrift

Twilight brings a time of day
When many creatures make their way
An Elephant in the failing light
With other creatures of the night.

Lions will be hunting soon
Warthogs feed beneath the moon
Hyenas laugh, and Jackals howl
And sawing Leopards are on the prowl.

These delights are but a few
The African bush can hold for you
To truly live a man must go
Where Buffalo roam, and the Kaffir trees grow.

Nature's balance is supreme
To better this is but a dream
This Eden that I have observed
Some caring people have preserved.

H. R. Plastow.

AWAKEN TO LIFE

Have you really looked around
And seen the beauties that abound
A field of grass has beauty true
But sad to say, is seen by few.

Have you ever watched the trees
Clouds scudding fast upon the breeze
The Autumn tints that turn to gold
As nature's wonders do unfold.

So **few** people realise
We live in such a paradise
All too often we don't see
The simple beauty of a tree.

Have you ever spent the hours
Walking in the fields of flowers
The Cowslip and the Oxlip too
And Bluebells oft enjoyed by few.

Flowers of the field may be
A sight that you may never see
Modern farming holds no place
For beauty, sentiment or grace.

Often people passing by
May only look with half an eye
Train the mind to really look
Do not miss the common Rook.

At evening have you ever stood
Beside a gate, or in a wood
And felt that life was all around
With call of Owl, and stranger sound.

If we take a while to dream
And for new pleasures do not scheme
Many things we may observe
And nature's pleasures we'll deserve.

Can you say you've ever seen
Weeds growing in a natural scene
Nature has a perfect plan
But this is often spoilt by man.

Look how tidy is the hill
Where heather grows, and time stands still
No weeds beneath the woodland trees
Ferns waving gently in the breeze.

Look upon the lonely moor
Where mosses grow, and Buzzards soar
The streams that murmur through the rocks
With darting Trout and stealthy Fox.

Have you seen the world arise
Stood beneath the lightening skies
Seen the Curlew lift at dawn
From tide's edge on a summer morn.

Wherever you or I may be
Many things we do not see
There's sick and lonely people who
Would like to pass an hour or two.

Some old people down the street
May struggle hard to make ends meet
A friendly word in passing by
May help to keep a tear from eye.

There are so many ways to look
Quite enough to write a book
Let's hope this poem has a way
To brighten up somebody's day.

H. R. Plastow

Chapter 29

INDIA – LAND OF MYSTERY

The continent of India, with its great distances, its timeless landscape, simple way of life and numerous Holy Men, has probably produced more tales of mystery than anywhere else on earth.

During a short stay in hospital, in November 1984, I was fortunate in meeting a Hindu gentleman, originally from the North East Region of India, before he came to live in England. His very personal experiences (at a difficult time in his life), relating to a sacred ceremony – the Sradh, give an insight into the Spiritual life of his country; and I am privileged to be able to describe them.

The eldest of six brothers, Rama was educated at Calcutta, and London Universities. He was just a young man when his father suddenly died of cholera, leaving him the responsibility of supporting the family. At the time I describe, 1942–1944, he worked at the Imperial Secretariat at Simla, and during the Second World War was employed by our government to monitor German and Japanese broadcasts.

About two years after the death of his father, Rama had married 'Chinu', a young Indian girl. They were extremely happy, going almost everywhere together, and every evening (when he was working), she would wait for him by the steps of The Secretariat.

One morning before leaving for work, Rama realised that his wife was not well, but they both thought this to be just a minor disorder. Later in the day, a neighbour contacted him to tell him to go straight to the hospital, where his wife had been admitted. On arrival, he found her unconscious, and seriously ill with double pneumonia. Unfortunately, she did not regain consciousness, and died on the following day; not yet seventeen, and no more than a year after her marriage to Rama.

Such a great loss is heart-rending for anyone, although time is usually a great healer, but for Rama, this was not to be. As the days passed by, he began to experience continuous nightmares, in which his wife would call, and beckon him to follow. They were so real that on several occasions he fell from his bed onto the floor as he moved in sleep, to try to follow her. The nightmares continued to be so vivid that sleep walking became an added problem.

During the two years of these nightmares, Rama would often see his wife sitting on a pouffe beside her bed, but if he expected to see her, or purposely looked, the apparition would disappear. Chinu had been aware that certain foods did not agree with her husband, and when they were out to dine, she would often put her hands together, momentarily, over a dish to indicate that this was not for him. Dining out one evening, after his wife had died, the meal was being served when he recognised the hands of his wife extended over the dish that had been put before him. There was no question, he recognised the hands, her rings, and bangles – these were those of his wife. In India, one does not look at the face of a married woman, but his eyes immediately followed the wrists to the arms, but these were not those of Chinu; and on looking back, the hands had changed to those of the serving woman. However, the dish was one that Rama would not normally eat.

One day, during the time that the nightmares persisted, and being exhausted through lack of sleep, Rama laid down on the sea wall at Chowpati, Bombay. No doubt the nightmare was causing him to be restless, when he fell off the sea wall some way down onto the stones below, knocking himself unconscious. Police were soon on the scene, and at first thought that he was drunk, but they were kind to him, and helped him back to his hotel.

Rama rested in the hotel, and at supper time on the evening of the second day he sat apart from the main group of people in the hall, because he did not feel well, having something of a headache, from the fall. As he sat on the floor, he became aware of a Pundit (a very learned priest), making his way through the crowd towards him. He seemed different to any other priest that he had seen before, and Rama heard people in the hall saying "A Saint is here, he looks different to other priests". The Pundit was dressed in the traditional yellow, saffron coloured robes, his head was shaven in the usual way of priests, and he carried a pathfinder (a stick), as tall as himself. In his left hand he held a brass jar, with a spout (a kamandalu), in which would be Holy water, which priests sprinkle as they go along their way.

The Holy Man came towards Rama, not looking into his eyes, but staring straight at his forehead. He said that he knew Rama was troubled, and that Rama's wife was unable to relinquish her association with him. He carried on to advise him to go to Panchabati and offer a Sradh, to try to satisfy the departed soul. He explained that this did not always work, but that it should for Rama. He told him that when he looked into the water at this Holy place, he might not see his wife, but as long as he saw a person of the same sex, then the offering of the Sradh **had** worked. The Pundit said that he must leave now, to pray. Rama asked where he could find him if he needed any more advice, and the priest replied that if Rama went to the Holy place; if he was lucky, he might see him again.

As the Pundit departed, Rama watched him pass through the crowd and make his way down the hotel steps to the street, but then saw him no more as he disappeared in the busy throng, outside the hotel.

Within a few days, Rama made the hundred mile train journey from Victoria Station Bombay, to Nasik Road, after which he caught a bus to make the four hour ride to Panchabati. This whole area is a sacred place, and the buses at that time were run on charcoal (presumably steam driven), and were quite slow, but helped to preserve the peace of the area. After leaving the bus, he walked barefoot to the sacred area of the Koshaborta.

The Holy place is in fact the source of the Godavari River. Koshaborta is an area of large Banyon trees, and many hills, from which numerous trickles of water make their way downhill to feed into a large natural basin, where the water is perfectly calm. The tepid water is thought to have healing properties, especially for skin complaints. From the outfall of this basin, begins one of the mightiest, and most sacred rivers of India, meandering over nine hundred miles, crossing the Deccan and flowing into the bay of Bengal. It is in the basin at Koshaborta that those who offer their Sradh must stand waist deep, and look into the water. The Sradh is made by the payment of money to the priests, the offer of flowers on the water, and the continuous prayer; and chanting by the priests and the burning of incense.

Before seeking absolution, it is necessary to fast, and then to take part in a ceremony. Rama asked the priests if it would be possible to see both his wife and father, but they told him that he could make his offering to one person only, otherwise it might not work; although other spirit persons might make themselves known.

With some apprehension, Rama walked out into the water to waist depth. He had been told not to look anywhere other than down into the water, and once he stopped, he remained quite still, looking straight down. Once the ripples ceased, he could see his own reflection, and in fact saw nothing more for almost two hours, when he had become somewhat shaky; keeping still for so long. Then, instead of his own reflection, he saw flowers appear in the water. When the picture of the flowers faded, they were replaced by the face of a woman; which then faded to be replaced by the face of his father, and eventually this was replaced by flowers, which soon disappeared to leave his own reflection in the water once again. After this ceremony, he felt uplifted, and that night slept soundly for the first time for a very long while, and having no further problems with sleep.

Feeling that a great worry had left him, and wishing to thank the Pundit, Rama felt a strong urge to find him. He made extensive enquiries of the priests at the Holy place, but they did not know of any such Pundit, and although they asked the name of the hotel where this priest had appeared, they could throw no light on his identity whatsoever. On going back to the area of the hotel, Rama made further enquiries, but no one had seen a priest of that description before, or since. He spent a lot of time, and money over several years trying to locate this Holy Man, but he had disappeared without trace.

There have been various accounts in which a person is seen in one place, although in fact is in another at the same time. One very seriously wonders in this instance if this is a similar occurrence. There are several factors which make it seem highly likely. Firstly, Bombay is an area with a large population, and one young man falling off a wall might be expected to cause little comment, especially two days after the event; yet the Holy Man suddenly makes his way through the crowd in the hotel, to go directly to Rama – when, to a stranger, he might have been anyone in the hall. Then, his disappearance, when **even** other priests did not know him. I enquired of Rama if at any time he had touched the Pundit, as I felt sure I knew the answer – very definitely, he had not.

It seems likely that this saintly priest may well have been sitting beneath a tree, perhaps hundreds of miles away, but being so spiritually developed, that he could project his conscious self, for the purpose of good. I have no experience of this type of manifestation, but if one studies the last paragraph of 'The Addendum to Chapter 26,' near the end of the book, we see a similar type of visitation, for good; although in this instance the man's father was in spirit, as indeed **The Holy Man may well have been**.

Chapter 30

ACCEPTANCE

By committing these various experiences to paper, I realise that there is infinitely more to life than we may appreciate. There would appear to be a wealth of help available, in the form of good advice, and healing if our lives make it possible to receive it. Perhaps we should try not to block the efforts of our friends (in a higher existence), by foolish conceit, greed and the desire for self esteem; these are products of an immature mind. 'For what shall it profit a man, if he shall gain the whole world, and lose his own soul?' Mark 8. Verse 6.

We are just ordinary people, perhaps differing from some in that money has never been our first consideration. Also, we feel that it is necessary for man to do a proper day's work for a sensible day's pay, based on his skills and effort; in order to preserve happiness; and believe that easy times and too many luxuries do not make contented people.

Our family has enjoyed the pleasures of the countryside, and are not against sport. However, one should not kill wantonly, or without consideration. The Bible tells us – 'Have dominion over the fish of the sea and over the fowl of the air, and over every living thing that moveth upon the earth' Although I am sure we should not abuse this privilege, taking only the surplus, and not persecuting any species to endanger its existence.

Over hundreds of years, there have been many accounts of supernatural activity. Many thousands of people (like ourselves), have received help through spiritual healers, and mediums, yet man in his conceit or fear of such matters has blotted out any real spiritual progress. Surprisingly, we can learn to fly, and in a relatively short space of time, can produce diabolical flying machines and missiles to kill our fellow man, and yet seem quite unable to learn, or make any real progress in any spiritual manner. This desirable progress should not be looked on as a matter of religion, but as an integral part of life itself!

It is a fact that the birds, the animals and all the creatures on this earth, could live and exist indefinitely without ever spoiling their environment, natural selection controlling the quality of life, and the numbers. One must believe that we were given reasoning power to make us superior to the animals and creatures of the earth. Unfortunately, our ability to think has made us inferior to them. Surely then, the creatures have a far greater right to live on this earth than us human beings – a very sobering thought. But after all they **could** live on indefinitely, but we very definitely **could not**.

I have often wondered if the lesson of life, is to accept what we have, and not to seek more. Once we try to create contrivances to minimise the work and maximise the profit, man's days are numbered on this earth. Certainly we can take a lesson from the creatures, and try and live in accord with nature, rather than to continually ruin our environment, in so many ways.

If man is absolutely honest, the good he has achieved is far outweighed by the bad, and his preoccupation with destroying his environment, and his fellow man, must surely count as the supreme failure of the human race!

There will be voices raised in protest; but it would seem that man without reasoning power and leading a simple life, could exist indefinitely, and without problems. Of course, there would not be the medical help available, in the normal sense, but this aspect would be far outweighed by the enormous numbers of human beings throughout the world, who would no longer be killed or maimed, by man's ceaseless wars and senseless creations!

Addendum to Chapter 26:

In her letter Olive says: "I have always felt sure that there **must** be something more than **this** life, and have had that feeling shown to be true, several times. My Mum – who died young, lost two babies and I was old enough to remember the second one and can remember Mum saying that she saw her baby's spirit go out of the bedroom window. (This type of manifestation has been recorded to be in the form of a moving light. Author.)

On another occasion, we had two cousins (some years older than I was) staying, and they walked to Rumburgh to visit another Aunt and Uncle; we lived at Ivy Cottage, St. James, it was a double dwelling then. The Aunt was ill, and when they came back to Ivy Cottage, they went upstairs to Mum who was a-bed with a new baby, and the first thing she said was 'You needn't tell me, I know Aunt Liza is dead'. When they asked how she knew, she said 'She came and stood by my bed', and it was the exact time of her death. My cousin told me of this in later years, and Mum also told me. At some time in her childhood Mum had lived with her Mother and Step Father in a farm in Rumburgh – (can't remember the name), and she awoke one night to find a woman with long hair, near her bed. She was frightened of course. The Cousin – Flo – mentioned above, lived in London, and used to come and stay with me in later years (she was fourteen years older than me) and we used to enjoy having her. She got interested in Spiritualism, and told us of one time she and her sister went to a meeting – the medium asked – did she know anyone called Sam. Flo couldn't recall anyone, and the medium said she definitely had a Sam, and he wanted to thank Flo and her family for the food and cigs. they had sent to him; also mittens. Then the penny dropped – Cousin Sam from Linstead, who was killed in the First World War! She was so pleased.

At one time (about 1937–38), we lived in a cottage in Beccles (this is my married life now) and we had next door but one, an elderly couple – well fiftyish to my 30! and they had a niece living with them. She had been in service and contracted rheumatic fever and was left crippled with arthritis. It got worse and worse, in spite of gold injections and all the rest. Flo – knew Ada of course, and asked for absent healing for her, and do you know, she improved from being able to do not one single thing for herself – to being able to eat her food using a fork, holding a cup of drink with both hands, doing up her buttons, and even doing a bit of simple embroidery. Eventually she was able to walk with sticks with places for her arms to rest in.

Did I imagine this? In the evening of the day of my first husband's funeral, a few of my family, and myself were sitting talking, and of course I was upset. I felt a pressure on my left shoulder. So real, I had to turn and see who it was. Was he comforting me? That same husband worked for Masters and Skevens of Beccles, plumbers and heating engineers. Jim was mate to an older man who had to leave a bit early to get to the Norwich train. Yes – that's a lot of years ago, nearly fifty I guess. The men didn't leave off till 6 p.m. However they were working at Roos Hall, Barsham just outside the Beccles boundary. Mr. Harris cycled off to catch his train and left Jim to lock up the hall, it being empty at that time. He locked up, and left for home and on turning to close the meadow gate, saw he had left the lights on. Well, he **knew** he hadn't but was going back to see, anyway. Before he could get back, the place was in darkness. We often used to try to work that one out, no street lights to throw reflections on to all those windows. Roos Hall has a bloodstain somewhere on a floor, which I was told could not be scrubbed out.

Another thing came to light recently. When one of my sisters had her third child, she was very near to death, and she has told me – Mum appeared at her bedside. Fortunately, both mother and baby are still living today.

When my second husband died, B.R. sent a very nice man to see if I needed help in any way, and if I had any family. We were speaking of this and that, and he said he firmly believed in after life. He said when his Dad died he came and visited him, and told him not to worry as he was quite happy. I heard **that** with a bit of disbelief; but since reading your book – I'm not so sure I was right in my opinion!"

O. Vickery.

CONCLUSION

After 50 years of psychic experience, and observation, it should be possible to form some opinions. I have wondered why these manifestations were shown to myself, and family, and have marvelled at the fact that the important experiences are so well corroborated. One asks, is there a definite purpose for these revelations, and is there some peculiarity of some people's lives which makes spiritual contact possible?

When our girls were very young, I would often say to them "You learn by keeping your mouth shut, and your ears open". One needs to be a good listener, and observe, to progress in any situation. I have been told on a number of occasions, that I am a good listener, and I suspect this ability is a main ingredient, not only for progress in this life, but is more specially needed for any spiritual contact to be able to take place. There is today, a tendency of many to wish to speak, but not to listen; perhaps because of the high pressure of modern living. Thus it may be possible for them to give knowledge, but not to receive it.

I cannot feel that I have any attributes to aid psychic contact, other than being a good listener. It seems logical that if one is able to listen and learn, in this life; then at times it may be possible for contact to come through from a higher existence. This would also explain why the family have become involved, because we are all basically the same sort of people. If one's mind is full of thoughts of one's own presumed importance, and the pursuit of material gains, then this more than anything seems to block out psychic contact. It is almost always the most simple unassuming persons, that are the more spiritually developed.

Our experiences tell something of hauntings, and apparitions, and it would seem that an apparition may appear repeatedly, in certain locations, in a projected – unaware form. As regards the manifestations at the Rectory, none were bothering, and almost all occurred within the first few years of our coming to the property.

I am convinced that the minds, and the personalities of people that live in a property, normally predominate, and thus manifestations will often discontinue. It would seem also, that a property left empty

The author with his original 'Bill' traction engine model, passes Roy Swain on 'Violet', at the Hastingwood Rally, 1962. Photo: B. J. Finch.

for a time, may well attract spirit entities, or projections from the past. Perhaps just like squatters, in an empty house; obviously there would be no adverse mental forces, as might well be present from living owners.

Spiritual contact, or projection; such as happened after our horse 'Goldie' died suddenly; would always seem possible, even likely, because in this instance he was taken suddenly in the prime of life. However, no contact has been observed from 'Ben' or 'Jane', no doubt because they have lived out their lives, in the normal way. There are many such examples, where a life is terminated unexpectedly. However, happy times or just strong associations with a place or person; or a spirit person wishing to help, would seem capable of producing a contact.*

The occurrences at the Rectory have been (I consider) both from the past and from more recent times. This house has always had an atmosphere of peace, and visitors have often remarked about this. Over the years, we have had a number of people stay, overnight, and without exception tell us what a good night's sleep they had enjoyed. The usual remark – "I slept like a log."

After the numerous experiences we have enjoyed, I can only say that one comes to accept them, and indeed to be very grateful for them when they sometimes concern healing powers, without which, all hope might have gone.

* Jane our mare, regrettably had to be put down in October 1984 (at the age of 29 years), having terminal colic.

FINIS

There is a quotation which says – 'The life of every man touches another'. When one considers the train of events which have been recorded in this book, this old saying seems very true.

Supposing I had never met Roy Swain, and in turn had not met Mr. Wesley, then my wife and I would not have met Kathleen St. George. Had I not worked with Eric Crowe, his life could not have become interwoven with ours in the contact with my brother.

In the same way one must consider how surprising it is that four people travelled through the same village at the same time of the evening, but in different years, and that each saw 'The little old lady', Chapter 16. Sightings are not common, and therefore it must be remarkable that Ron May, and the other persons are known to me, so that each learns of the other's experience. Perhaps these things are pre-ordained as suggested in the Foreword – like the Arab belief – 'It is written'.

But for all these events, this book would not have been written. If our family story has encouraged just a few people to take a more reasonable view and accept those in the spirit world; then our efforts, and those of our friends in 'Class A', will not have been in vain.

H.R.P.

NOTES: Healing ability may be dormant in many of us. A healer is believed to be a channel through which healing powers are conveyed from those in spirit. There have been several very famous healers, and those healing directly by the laying on of hands, may be better known. Genuine healers claim no credit for the benefits they help to achieve, considering themselves only as an instrument.

Absent healing is less known, but many believe this to be the more powerful form. This is generally achieved by contacting a healing group, by letter, and enclosing a photograph of the person or creature requiring help; perhaps yourself or someone else – who does not even need to know. Prayer, and thought from the healers can be very beneficial, as one realises from this book, but like all forms of healing, it cannot always work. The healers carry out their services for the love of helping humanity, and do not ask for reward. However, in consideration of their good work, small donations help to keep it available for others.

'Publications – H. R. Plastow'

Specialised books or booklets by the same publisher:

The Building and Running of Steam Traction Engine and Roller Models

THE BURRELL BUILDERS BOOK OF PICTURES

THE FOWLER BUILDERS BOOK OF PICTURES

How To Get The Best From Your MODEL TRACTION ENGINE

By H. R. Plastow